D0604661

THE
TEDDY BEAR
BOOK

THE
TEDDY BEAR
BOOK

Maureen Stanford
and Amanda O'Neill

JG
PRESS

CLB 3327
Published in the USA 1995 by JG Press.
Distributed by World Publications, Inc
Copyright © 1994 by CLB Publishing Ltd,
Godalming, Surrey

All rights reserved
No part of this book may be reproduced or transmitted in any
form or by any means, electronic or mechanical,
including photocopying, recording, or by any
information storage and retrieval system,
without permission in writing from
the Publisher

Printed and bound in Singapore
ISBN 1-57215-054-8

The JG Press imprint is a
trademark of JG Press, Inc.
455 Somerset Avenue,
North Dighton, MA 02764

Consultant: Hamish MacGillivray
Managing Editor: Jo Finnis
Editor: Adèle Hayward
Photography: Neil Sutherland
Photographic Assistance: Nigel Duffield
Design: Phil Clucas
Illustration: Kevin Jones Associates
Typesetting: Mary Wray
Production: Ruth Arthur; Sally Connolly; Neil Randles;
Karen Staff; Jonathan Tickner
Director of Production: Gerald Hughes

The teddy bears and the patterns and instructions for
'Making An Heirloom Bear' on pp. 140–153 were supplied
by Mary Holden of 'Only Natural', Tunbridge Wells, Kent.

CONTENTS

❤

Bears with a mission: Barnaby and Junior sort out their equipment for the Grand Tour. Next, Barnaby has to study the family tree to decide which relatives to visit where, and in which order. It looks as though Junior's ploy to dodge his lessons is going to bear fruit in a way he didn't expect. If Barnaby has his way, the youngster will end up a very well-educated bear indeed. Perhaps he will qualify to set up as a cub reporter on the strength of his travels!

Barnaby is well qualified for the role of guide through Bearland. He bears his knowledge lightly, but he has a degree in Teddiology from Bearmingham University.

INTRODUCTION

With Barnaby Through Bearland

I t was a glorious day; not the sort of day for a young bear to sit indoors and have lessons. "I can't bear history," murmured Junior sadly, as his uncle Barnaby explained how the great Columbear discovered America. Barnaby is a very well-read bear – rather too well-read, Junior reckons – and he just loves sharing his knowledge. Junior wondered how to deflect his tutor. "I know!" he cried suddenly. "Uncle Barnaby, let's go on a Grand Tour of Beardom! If we make a tour of all our relatives, we can do history and geography and genealogy and bearology and enjoy ourselves at the same time!" Barnaby was dubious. He suspected Junior's motives. But the youngster brought all his powers of persuasion to bear, and gradually Barnaby began to perceive the advantages of his scheme. Yes, he concluded, Junior would certainly benefit from discovering his forebears and meeting some of the great figures of teddy history – as well as the rising stars of today. Perhaps they could visit a teddy hospital so Junior could study the inner bear, maybe watch an operation or two – though Barnaby himself felt a bit squeamish about the more intimate details of bear care and repair. "All right," he declared, "let's go!"

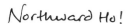

"I'm packed, Uncle Barnaby!" cries Junior. "I didn't mean you to pack yourself in the bag, you foolish bear!" scolds Barnaby. But Junior is only joking. At last everything is ready and, as Junior flings his hat in the air with joy, the two bears set off.

Northward Ho!
We've just sailed through
the Bearing Straits.
We didn't 'paws' for a
chat with our Polar cousins,
though — 'fur' too cold!
Regards —
Barnaby and
Junior

The Bruin Family
7 Steiff Avenue
Chad Valley
Bear Island

THE TEDDY BEAR STORY

Ancestors Of The Teddy Bear

"Are you sitting comfortably?" asked Barnaby. "I'm so excited I can bearly sit still," replied Junior. "Let's begin at the beginning." "A good place!" his nephew agreed. "Bears have always been important to humans even since ancient times," said Barnaby. "Perhaps because they walk upright, perhaps because they sometimes behave like humans – clowning around or having a temper tantrum," "I never have tantrums," said Junior. Barnaby looked doubtful. "Many ancient peoples believed bears and humans were related," he went on. "Native Americans honoured the bear as their ancestor, while European legends tell of the Bear Son, a half man, half bear endowed with supernatural strength."

ABOVE LEFT: The carved bear on this Native American pipe is a sacred image which often appeared in drawings on masks or totem poles.

ABOVE RIGHT: When pulled along, weights on the foot of this bear make it dance. Long before the creation of the teddy bear, naturalistic model bears, often mounted on wheels, were popular in the nursery.

American Beginnings

"The birth of the teddy bear in America is irrevocably linked with President Roosevelt's hunting expedition in November 1902." "Wasn't his nickname 'Teddy'?" piped in Junior. "Well done," Barnaby congratulated him. "He was paying an official visit to Mississippi to settle a Mississippi-Louisiana boundary dispute. He went on a shooting expedition, but refused to kill a young black bear. *Washington Star* cartoonist Clifford Berryman sketched the incident, making it a metaphor for the President's political mission. Few political cartoons have achieved such lasting fame! The teddy became a political icon – and astute toymakers leapt on the bandwagon. Russian immigrant Morris Michtom is thought to have been first in the field with a stuffed toy bear made by his wife – tradition says it was he who obtained the President's permission to market his toys as 'Teddy's bears'".

RIGHT: Berryman's cute, big-eared bear is far from naturalistic, and gave toymakers the cue to transform the bear into the teddy.

LEFT: Now in the Smithsonian Institute, Washington DC, this is said to be one of the original bears made by the Ideal and Novelty Toy Company, founded by Morris Michtom.

THE TEDDY BEAR STORY

German Beginnings

"In the same year that Roosevelt didn't shoot his bear, in Germany Richard Steiff invented a jointed bear-doll. German toy manufacturers had a long-established tradition of naturalistic toy bears, and the Steiff company, founded by Richard's aunt Margarete, had a successful line in wheeled bears. Richard's invention was exported to New York in February 1903, but failed to take the buyers' fancy." "I suppose they were bearly even interested," said Junior. "Only a month later, however," Barnaby went on, "the Steiff *Bärle* became a hit at the 1903 Leipzig Spring Fair. United States wholesalers, jumping on the Roosevelt mascot bandwagon, ordered a large batch, and from then on demand was so high that the Steiff company describe the next five years as the *Bärenjahre*, the 'bear years'. Bear historians still argue whether the first teddies were the all-American product of Morris Michtom, or German Steiff imports. They were soon to become universal!

TOP, FAR LEFT: Margaret Steiff began as a dressmaker, later extending her range into stuffed animals. Her first toy was an elephant pincushion!
TOP LEFT: Her nephew, Richard Steiff joined the company in 1879.
FAR LEFT: An extremely rare early Steiff made of white cotton plush.
LEFT: Factories in Germany could soon hardly keep up with demand. In 1908 Steiff alone produced one million bears.

President Roosevelt: Father Of The Teddy Bear

"Theodore Roosevelt was an active outdoors type and big-game hunter – hence his 1902 bear hunt. He was also a conservationist, who founded America's first national wildlife refuge," said Barnaby. "Did he have any pets?" asked Junior. "Yes," said Barnaby. "More than any other US president! Today he is remembered for raising and commanding 'Roosevelt's Roughriders', the first US volunteer cavalry – and for giving his name to the world's best loved toy. He used teddies as campaign mascots, though his daughter reported he never really cared for them!"
"It's difficult to believe that Teddy couldn't bear teddies!" Junior cried.

RIGHT: Roosevelt poses in Roughrider uniform, as does a miniature bear, said to have been a table favour at Roosevelt's inauguration ball in 1905. Roosevelt was quick to recognize the value of his popular mascot, which appeared on items from campaign buttons to this early toy drum, depicting the President mounted on a bear and leading the way.

THE TEDDY BEAR STORY

Teddy Bear Memorabilia

"From its beginnings as a political mascot, the bear has spread to every walk of life. He was the obvious motif for children's clothing, bedding, furniture, nursery china and cutlery," said Barnaby. "To say nothing of teething rings, hot water bottle covers and, of course, storybooks. "In adult life teddies became equally prevalent. The fashionable pre-war lady might secure her hat with a silver teddy hatpin, clip on a jewelled teddy brooch, and tuck into her handbag miniature teddies containing perfume spray and powder compact. From jigsaws to ashtrays, from postcards to matchboxes, the teddy bear crops up everywhere. The range is endless – and continually expanding."

TOP LEFT: For a pre-war baby, a teething rattle with a sterling silver bear above a mother-of-pearl handle. Many such rattles also sport jingling bells.

LEFT: The teddy cup and plate with bears playing soccer and golf were exported from Germany to England in the 1930s.

RIGHT: More recent collectables include brooches such as these – fully jointed, gold-plated bears studded with faux citrines and with faux emerald eyes.

Advertising Teddies

"Bears have always been popular emblems," said Barnaby. "Can you think of any names meaning 'bear'?" "What about Bruno, Bernard or Bjorn," said Junior. "Yes, and Arthur and Ursula. In the Middle Ages, bears featured on coats of arms and inn signs. Their modern relatives pose as emblems of sports teams, like Chicago's football team, known since 1922 as 'The Bears'. They are also common as trademarks, and have been used to sell everything from soap to lettuce! The invention of the teddy led a number of manufacturers to metamorphose their bear logos into teddy logos. During the height of the teddy craze, teddy bears entered the commercial world in a big way. Manufacturers boosted sales by offering teddy bears as give-aways in return for box tops or labels, and many of these are highly valued today, from the 1920s Bear Brand Hosiery 'cut and sew' bears to the 1958 Clairol vinyl-faced bear and the 1971 Maxwell House Coffee teddy.

ABOVE LEFT: Teddy bears have had a great career in advertising! This illustrated bear was offered as a give-away to readers of the American magazine Woman's Home Journal *who introduced six new subscribers.*

ABOVE RIGHT: The bear itself, able to trace its lineage back to that magazine advertisement in the 1920s.

LEFT: The top-hatted teddy became the trademark of Bear Brand hosiery in the 1930s, displacing a naturalistic bear image.

THE TEDDY BEAR STORY

Man's Best Friend

"People loved teddies from the start," said Barnaby. "I'm not surprised at that," said Junior. "We're great." "Humans obviously think so," agreed Barnaby. "No other toy has ever rivalled the bear's widespread popularity, durability or social acceptability among adults as well as children. No other toy so persistently acquires a history and personality of its own. Grown-ups who have 'put aside childish things' feel no need to discard their teddies, but keep them into old age. It is hard to explain teddy power. As a toy, the teddy combines the virtues of doll and stuffed animal, and appeals to both girls and boys, but there is more to it than that. As collectables, teddies have the advantage of great character. They all share similar basic features, but, like people, show marked individuality. But that isn't everything. Teddy bears represent security, comfort and friendship." "So people can't bear to be parted from them," Junior declared.

TOP RIGHT AND FAR RIGHT: No picture of family life would be complete without the essential bear, and equally, the bear is part of our image of childhood.

RIGHT: Peter Bull was the first celebrity bear collector. Since then, teddy bear rallies, teddy bear picnics and teddy museums have sprung up for the benefit of bear lovers.

ABOVE: 'Peter', on the box, and 'Happy', seen with owner Rosemary Volpp, are golden oldies. 'Peter' (1925) is a rare breed. Few were sold, and collectors were thrilled at the discovery of a cache of unsold stock. "Happy has a very pretty face," blushed Junior. "Her owners thought so," said Barnaby. "I'm sure it was that and her scarcity value that made her the world's most expensive bear. But collectors also value modern teddies like the miniature Steiff leaning on Peter's box."

The Teddy Bear Collector

"Teddy bear collecting – arctophilia – began in the 1970s, when old bears began to be valued as antiques. Early bears have risen hugely in value. In 1989 collectors Rosemary and Paul Volpp paid a record price of £55,000 ($86,350) for an early Steiff called 'Happy'." "That must have made her even happier," said Junior. "Few collectors are in it for the money, though. Bear collecting became respectable in 1969, thanks to actor Peter Bull. The owner of 250 bears, Bull researched the role of teddy bears in people's lives and wrote *The Teddy Bear Book*." "So other people admitted they collected teddies, too," said Junior. "Yes, and many new collectors took up the hobby. Today, arctophiles all over the world share their interests at bear conventions, subscribe to specialist journals, visit teddy bear museums as far flung as Florida, Queensland or Stratford-upon-Avon, and celebrate 'Good Bear Day' on President Roosevelt's birthday, 27th October."

THE INNER BEAR

Bear Beginnings

"To understand bear history," Barnaby explained, "we need to be familiar with the basic facts of life." "You mean where bears come from and how they are made?" asked Junior. "Back to the factory and all that?" "That's right," Barnaby said. "So we'll start with a quick run down on factories and fabrics, stuffings and squeakers, and so on."

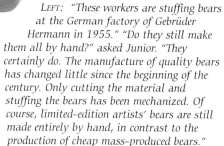

LEFT: "These workers are stuffing bears at the German factory of Gebrüder Hermann in 1955." "Do they still make them all by hand?" asked Junior. "They certainly do. The manufacture of quality bears has changed little since the beginning of the century. Only cutting the material and stuffing the bears has been mechanized. Of course, limited-edition artists' bears are still made entirely by hand, in contrast to the production of cheap mass-produced bears."

FABRICS: Bears have been made in every practicable material. The classic fabric, used for the first bears, is mohair plush (the wool of the Angora goat), which has a realistic texture and is highly resistant to dirt. Over the years, manufacturers experimented with cheaper materials such as cotton plush – and there was even a wartime economy fibre woven from nettles! More successful were synthetic fabrics, especially the 1930s invention of nylon, which was washable and could be dyed in a range of hues.

LEFT: It's hard to believe, said Junior, "that these bears have been made in the same pattern. The four fabrics used make them look so different!"

THE INNER BEAR

LEFT: Natural fabrics (from left to right): string mohair, German Zotty pile, feathered white mohair, German tipped mohair, curly mohair, straight mohair, short pile mohair, distressed mohair.

TOP RIGHT: Synthetic fabrics (from left to right): long pile synthetic plush, curly finish viscose, short pile synthetic plush, white polyester.

RIGHT: Paw pad materials show equal variety (from left to right): rexine, beige and dark brown felts, beige and golden brown suedette, yellow suede and black velveteen.

PAW AND FOOT PADS: Most early bears had pads cut from felt, or sometimes suede, a rather expensive material for a soft toy. In the 1930s a cheap wartime substitute was rexine, a fabric like oil cloth. They also sometimes used natural leather and velveteen. Later pads were made in plush, either incorporated with the limbs or with inserts of a contrast colour. Today washable synthetics are widely used.

STUFFING: Wood wool, a straw substance otherwise known as excelsior, was the earliest stuffing and remained in use for many years. After World War I kapok, a soft fibre made from the seed pods of the kapok tree, became the most popular alternative. Wartime bears had economy stuffings such as 'sub', waste from cotton mills. Bears from the war period have even been found stuffed with cut-up stockings. In the 1950s people wanted washable stuffings. Wood wool was no good, but shredded plastic foam proved even worse, as it broke down into sticky powder. Today, both traditional and modern materials, such as polyester wadding and plastic pellets, are used as stuffing.

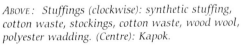

ABOVE: Stuffings (clockwise): synthetic stuffing, cotton waste, stockings, cotton waste, wood wool, polyester wadding. (Centre): Kapok.

FAR RIGHT: Pellets are a popular stuffing for the modern artist bear.

RIGHT: The fibre used for stuffing affects the look and character of the bear. Compare the stiff, upright early Steiff, stuffed with unyielding wood wool, with the softer, floppy 1992 bear on the far right who is stuffed with plastic pellets.

THE INNER BEAR

JOINTS: Early bears could move their heads, arms and hips quite freely. They had a card or metal disc inserted in either side of the joint. These were linked by a cotter or split pin fastened off with a small metal washer. Wire jointing was experimented with early on but this tended to give way easily with wear. Plastic rods replaced split pins in the 1940s and today cardboard joints have been replaced by plastic, although hardboard joints are still used for some artist bears. Over the years some manufacturers have economized by limiting jointing to the limbs or head only – so some bears could either walk or shake their heads, but not both.

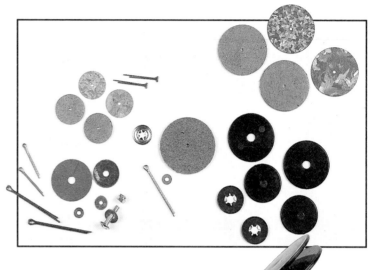

LEFT, RIGHT AND ABOVE: Bearmakers have long striven to find the perfect joint: (Left) Hardboard joints with cotter pins used for artist bears. (Right) Modern plastic joints.(Above, clockwise) Metal, metal and card, hardboard (centre), and plastic joints.

GROWLERS: The earliest voice box of the teddy bear was a reed in an oil cloth bag tied at each end. Squeezing or punching the bear allowed air to flow through the reed, making a quite peculiar noise. Squeakers (previously used on other toys) were also tried, but the tilt growler produced the true teddy voice. This growler consisted of a cardboard tube containing a small pair of bellows attached to a reed. When the bear was turned over, a lead weight at one end opened the bellows; when the bear was stood upright, it closed them again, giving a much slower, realistic noise. The principle of this growler is still used today.

BELOW: An array of growlers and squeakers gives some idea of the range of bear voices. (From left to right) punch growler, tilt growlers from the early 1900s, the 1930s (porcelain), the 1960s and the 1990s, and two variations of the modern plastic squeaker.

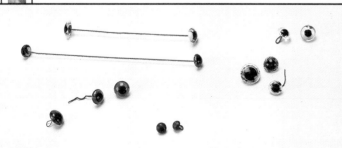

EYES: The first teddy bears were fitted with wooden shoe button eyes. In the 1900s a lady's boot might need 12 to 15 buttons, so there was a good supply. Larger bears needed purpose-made large buttons. Glass eyes were available but were not used for teddy bears until 1910 – and not universally accepted until after World War I.

LEFT: An assortment of eyes, including traditional shoe buttons eyes (centre front) and glass eyes with wire shanks or hooks.

THE INNER BEAR

The first glass eyes, imported from Germany, were of blown glass, brown with black pupils, but it soon proved cheaper to paint colour on the back. At first, eyes were fitted with a small metal hook at the back, but time was saved by placing an eye on each end of a long piece of wire which the seamstress could cut and bend as required. After World War II, government safety regulations led to the development of plastic eyes, at first sewn in place but later secured with a washer.

ABOVE: (Clockwise): Amber and black glass eyes from the 1960s, black and black and brown plastic saftey eyes, and plastic replica shoebutton eyes..

RIGHT: Early shoebutton eye on red felt, 1930s celluloid 'googly' eye, 1950s revolving plastic eye, and 1950s green glass eye.

NOSES: Many experiments were tried to achieve a natural looking nose. Leather and natural plastic (gutta percha) proved to be too hard, and hand-embroidered noses became the norm. Noses are a useful clue to a bear's manufacturer, as different firms favoured different shapes, such as triangular, elongated and round, and either vertical or horizontal stitching. Black rubber noses were introduced in 1945 and by the 1950s were widely used. Today, children's toys sport lock-in safety noses in plastic, while collectors' bears retain the traditional hand-sewn nose.

ABOVE AND LEFT: 1906 horizontally stitched Steiff nose, c. 1905 Steiff sealing wax nose, c. 1906 Ideal twill nose, 1920s Character metal nose, 1950s English plastic nose, and 1990s artist bear nose.

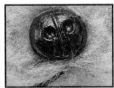

MOUTHS: Mouths are traditionally hand stitched, with a single line running from the centre of the nose to finish with an inverted V. Changing the shape of the V means bears can have very different expressions, from an upturned smile to a sad face. Occasionally bears were made with open mouths with felt lining and sometimes a tongue. Teeth proved an unpopular addition and are rare.

RIGHT: Much of a bear's expression depends on the mouth. (Clockwise): The classic inverted V-shaped stitched nose, a more aimiable wide-stitched smiling mouth, the moulded teeth of the German 'Peter Bear', a friendly lop-sided grin from a traditional shaped mouth, and the appealing T-shaped stitching of an early Ideal bear.

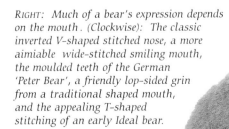

AMERICAN TEDDY BEARS

Thank You, Mr President!

"Our conquest of the United States began, as you'll remember," said Barnaby, "in November 1902, when President 'Teddy' Roosevelt, a keen hunter, refused to shoot the helpless bear cub. Bears were in the news, and in March 1903 a New York importer, George Borgfeldt and Co., ordered 3,000 Steiff bears from Germany. Later that same year, Morris and Rose Michtom of New York were inspired to market their own version of 'Teddy's Bear'." "And so we got our name!" squeaked Junior. "Precisely," said Barnaby. "And we bear it with pride, for it was inspired by a presidential act of mercy. Maybe that was why teddies became popular so quickly. Toymakers had produced bears before, but merely as part of a range of stuffed animals. The new cuddly teddy bears took the country by storm. By 1907 makers in most major American cities were working full out to meet the demand for teddies – and claiming their toys were quite as good as the European imports. Early American bears explored a wide variety of styles and included a quite startling range of novelties, including a Self-whistling Bear, a Topsy-turvy Bear, an Antiseptic Bear – and an Electro Bear with flashing eyes." "Shall we meet many of our early relatives?" asked Junior. "Not as many as I would wish," said Barnaby. "Many of the early makers were in production for only a short time, and their teddies are now very hard to find."

LEFT: *At the Carrousel Museum, Michigan, Mama and Baby Bear wait for Papa to complete a set made in the 1930s. America specialized in dressed bears as early as 1906, and demand remained strong into the 1930s. Integral clothes and bodies were popular in the 1920s-1930s.*

RIGHT: *The Dreamland Doll Company's Topsy-turvy doll (c. 1907) combines a gold mohair teddy, with jointed head and arms, and black Babyland Rag-type doll. It is now a very rare item.*

American Bear, c. 1920

American bears of the early 1900s are far less standardized than their German and British counterparts, although certain characteristic features soon emerged by which they may be distinguished. This early American bear is a typical example.

HEAD Short-snouted and rounder than in European bears, this bear also has large, wide-set ears. The rectangular nose is appliquéd black or dark brown twill, although many early American bears have a stitched nose. The mouth is embroidered in coarse floss in an inverted Y, curved at the ends in a particularly cheerful smile. The eyes are brown glass with black pupils.

BODY Almost humpless, with slightly roached back, and longer and narrower than the German and British styles. The shape is more doll-like than realistically ursine. Extremely hard wood wool stuffing gives this bear a rigid posture.

ARMS Short and fairly straight. This bear has a marked upward curve at the wrists so that his paws turn jauntily upwards as if to invite a hug, but many American bears of this period have no curve to the arm at all. The paws end in thin felt pads, somewhat worn, and they have never been endowed with claws.

FUR Short gold plush, remarkably well preserved despite the signs of wear on pads and feet.

LEGS Long and extremely straight, narrowing only slightly at the ankle and ending in small stubby feet with minimal shaping. For the portrait on the left, this elderly gentlebear is sensibly – or perhaps out of vanity – covering up the deficiencies of his poor pads with a cosy pair of bootees!

The Roosevelt Bears

The Roosevelt Bears, Teddy B (black or brown) and Teddy G (grey), were created in 1905 by children's writer Seymour Eaton as heroes of a series of rhyming tales. Adult educators scorned them, but children loved them, and they remained popular until World War I. Spin-offs included postcards, chinaware and board games. The Roosevelt Bears featured here are a modern reproduction in plush by D&D Productions of Maryland.

AMERICAN TEDDY BEARS

You Can't Beat A Bear!

When Roosevelt lost the presidency in 1909, toymakers expected 'Teddy's bear' to join him on the way out and hastily tried to come up with a successor. Several new stuffed toys were groomed for stardom, including 'Billy Owlett' (in patriotic dress) and 'Billy Possum' (referring to the new President Tate's enjoyment of a Georgia dinner of 'possum and 'taters'). "But none of them are remembered, while the ranks of teddies march on!" cheered Junior. "True," said Barnaby. "From the late 1970s, toymakers recognized a bear-collecting boom and started producing ranges specifically for collectors, often clearly marked 'not for children'. Many firms produced limited-edition bears, and this trend soon gave rise to the production of replicas of past models for collectors unable to afford the astronomically priced originals. Also, teddy bear artists began to produce meticulously crafted hand-made bears, designed to become the antiques of tomorrow. Examples of many of these modern bears, as well as their ancestors, are displayed at several teddy bear museums, or can be found at the teddy bear conventions held all over the United States." "I'd love to go to one," said Junior.

LEFT: LoneStar Bear, born in 1988, is hero of a storybook series. A simple Idaho mountain bear, he wants nothing more than to spend his time fishing, but is interrupted by adventures which take him around the world and even into space.

RIGHT: His soft fur, a blend of distressed silk and mohair, looks made for cuddles. But this 1992 bear is for collectors, not children. 'Master Witney' was made in a limited edition of only ten by teddy bear artist Pamela Wooley.

Two For The Price Of One

Found at the Portobello Road Flea market in London, there was something about this knitted ted that an intrepid teddy bear collector just knew was special. Underneath the immaculately knitted outer skin emerged a patched and repatched, but perfectly-formed, 1920s bear. Buttonholes had even been knitted to accommodate the original eyes.

AMERICAN TEDDY BEARS

ABOVE: To collectors, all bears are precious, not just the expensive ones. This quartet are mass-produced contemporary Californian College Bears, not of particularly high quality but valued as mascots.

BELOW RIGHT: The 'Heartful Dodger' is a 1992 limited-edition collectable made by Colorado teddy bear artist Diane Gard.

BELOW LEFT: Both humble mascots and fine artist bears find a welcome at the Carrousel Museum, Michigan, where Terry and Doris Michaud house more than 2,100 bears and produce their own hand-crafted, traditional-style teddies.

Brothers In Adversity

Teddy bears, unlike many other toys, are often the treasured companions of a lifetime. Consequently, many of the inmates of teddy bear museums have touching stories to tell of the owners they have outlasted. This pair of brothers, cuddling together for comfort, preserve the memory of an American family's wartime sufferings. The little fellow in the blue bow was the comforter of a lady whose husband was killed in World War II. His big brother, wearing a Roosevelt campaign button in honour of the man who inspired the creation of teddy bears, belonged to their son, who was killed in the Korean War. Both bears are American, but the makers are unknown. Only the history of the family who loved them remains.

IDEAL NOVELTY & TOY Co.

A Bright Idea Becomes An Ideal

"What happened to Morris Michtom after he produced his 'Teddy's bear'?" demanded Junior. "I am pleased to be able to tell you he went on to great things," Barnaby said. "Family tradition says he received President Roosevelt's approval to call his toy bears 'Teddy', but sadly there is no documentary evidence for this. However, Mr Michtom made more bears, and in 1903 their success enabled him to found the Ideal Novelty Toy Company – from 1938 known simply as the Ideal Toy Company. The firm prospered, and in 1908 was advertised as the 'Largest Bear Manufacturer in the Country'. By the 1960s they had factories in New York, Canada, Australia, New Zealand, Japan, Britain and Germany. In 1982 Mr Michtom's grandson sold the company, and two years later it stopped producing bears." "And what does the 'Ideal' bear look like?" Junior wanted to know. "Well," Barnaby explained, "they can be hard to identify since the firm seems not to have gone in for tags or labels." "The bear with no tag," murmured Junior. "That must make for problems." "It can do," Barnaby agreed, "for early Ideals are very similar to Steiff bears in design, and can be mistaken for them. Indeed, they have sometimes been mistakenly sold as Steiffs. But collectors who know what to look for can recognize them with a fair degree of confidence by certain distinguishing family characteristics. These include a triangular face, large ears set very low on the head and unique pointed toes.

"It's not often one can describe one's relations as ideal," Junior wisecracked, "but these American cousins fit the bill!"

BELOW LEFT: By 1915 Ideal bears had changed shape. This 1920s example shows the longer, oval, almost humpless body, shorter limbs and stubbier feet characteristic of later Ideal models.

BELOW RIGHT: In contrast, early Ideal bears like this fellow from c. 1910–1912 have a shorter, fatter body, much longer limbs and bigger feet. But facial features and expression retain a strong family resemblance.

IDEAL NOVELTY & TOY Co.

Ideal Bear, 1906-1907

Early Ideal bears may suffer a mild identity crisis since they were not provided with tags or labels. They can be recognized by design details such as the typical triangular head and unusual pointed foot pads.

HEAD This is one of the key identifying factors for early Ideals. It is typically large, with broad, rounded brow, steep forehead and the tell-tale triangular face. The muzzle is long, straight and wedge-shaped, while the endearingly quizzical expression adds to the bear's appeal – and to his collectability.

EARS Large, slightly cupped, wide set, and positioned noticeably low on the sides of the head.

HUMP The Steiff-like humped back is typical of early Ideals.

ARMS Long, with a marked curve at the wrist. Large paws with cotton pads and five claws.

LEGS Long (some early Ideals have shorter legs) with large feet. This bear lacks the pointed toes associated with the Ideal family.

LEFT: 'Cool Cat', a pre-1910 Ideal bear, reclines in the lap of his girlfriend 'No No Nanette', of the same period and probabaly also Ideal.

NOSE Appliquéd twill fabric – but horizontally stitched noses are just as characteristic of Ideal bears of this period.

EYES Round, shiny, black shoe-button eyes are typical of pre-World War I bears. The Ideal family have the eyes characteristically deepset. After the war, Ideal, like other firms, adopted the use of glass eyes.

BODY Long and narrow, in short golden mohair plush with a centre seam. The stuffing is wood wool, traditionally used for soft toys of the period.

IDEAL NOVELTY & TOY Co.

LEFT: Triangular faces tell us these two well-preserved elderly gentlebears are almost certainly Ideals. Vance, modelling the smart waistcoat, dates from c. 1908. His felt pads betray some wear but otherwise he is very fit for his age. Henry, in the hat, is a couple of years his junior.

Buddy

Buddy's wistful look suggests bittersweet memories of his own buddy, who fell in World War II. Buddy, a 1930 Ideal bear, and his American serviceman owner came to Britain in 1945 and were stationed at Burtonwood US Airbase near Warrington in Lancashire. The young man became engaged to a local girl, and Buddy remained with her when his owner left to take part in the D-Day landings. They waited in vain for the young man, but he was killed in action. His fiancée treasured Buddy all her life, and after her death in 1983 he retired to a teddy bear museum.

IDEAL NO____ TOY Co.

ABOVE: "Let me introduce you to this Ideal family," said Barnaby. "From left to right this is Elmer (pre-1910), Louie (1910-1914) and Monty (1904). His grey glass eyes were quite common in this period. Then there's Alastair (1906) and James (1906-1910).

BELOW LEFT: Furry Frankie from c. 1905, has a specially cuddly coat of gorgeous, long, silky mohair plush, and has an embroidered, rather than appliquéd, nose in black floss.

IDEAL NOVELTY & TOY Co.

BELOW: A patriotic bear of c. 1912 has the longer body and shorter limbs of the later Ideal bear.

FAR RIGHT: His older brother from c.1910 displays the pointed toes unique to Ideal.

RIGHT: The youngest brother, a 1940s model, is an Electric Eye Teddy. "Can I squeeze his chest?" asked Junior. "Go on," said Barnaby. His eyes contain light bulbs which flash. He also has an unusual open mouth, lined with felt.

ABOVE: Three bears spanning a range of years. Dennis in dungarees and Gregory, in the green jumper, date from 1915-1925. Nathan, in the necktie, dates from 1926-1932. Note that their pads have been replaced.

IDEAL NOVELTY & TOY Co.

ABOVE: Reginald, a 1920s bear in gold mohair, is believed to belong to the Ideal family. He is much longer in the body and shorter in the arms than earlier Ideals, but the low-set ears and prominent wedge-shaped muzzle remain true to the family ideal!

Smokey The Bear

In 1944 the US Forest Fire Prevention Campaign began promoting their cause with a character called Smokey the Bear. He was such a success that in 1953 Ideal began marketing a Smokey Bear soft toy. The first Smokey Bears, as seen here, have moulded vinyl faces and paws, a feature adopted by several bear-makers as early as the 1930s. Later Smokeys, made by Ideal and from the 1960s by other American manufacturers, reverted to the traditional plush. Toy Smokeys did their bit to increase children's awareness of the need to prevent forest fires. Young purchasers could become Junior Forest Rangers via the Ideal company. Later, Knickerbocker's 'talking' Smokeys had built-in tapes which told them directly about the campaign.

KNICKERBOCKER TOY Co. Inc.

From Nickname To Knickerbocker Glory!

"Let's have a success story now," Junior suggested. "Tell me about a firm which sailed on for years and years." "I was just about to do so," Barnaby said. "Let's turn to the Knickerbocker Toy Co. Inc." "What a funny name!" laughed Junior. "It's because this was a New York company," Barnaby explained. "New Yorkers were nicknamed 'Knickerbockers', from the baggy trousers of the original Dutch settlers. The company began making toys in 1850, and did not turn to teddy bears until the 1920s – but they went on producing them until the 1980s. Over those 60 years, of course, Knickerbocker bears changed and developed like those of other American firms, from early long-nosed models to flattened muzzles. Distinguishing features include large noses and ears – and a pride in their high quality of manufacture. They were even marketed as 'Animals of Distinction'. In the 1960s the firm produced highly successful Smokey Bears, including the 'talking' version."

BELOW: This 1920s-1930s bear wears his mohair with a difference. The bold contrast of golden eyes and nose against rich dark fur, and the unusually low-set ears create an unconventional appearance. But clearly his owner recognized the true bear character behind that rather stern gaze, for his brown velveteen pads are distinctly worn, and lovingly if inexpertly darned.

ABOVE: Two early Knickerbocker bears still have plenty of get up and go in them! Fergus, on the left, in the unusual yellowy-green mohair, sports a pair of boots just made for walking. From the state of his feet, his pal Pedro should have followed suit! Pedro's label has gone the way of his foot fur, but the family ears help to identify him.

KNICKERBOCKER TOY Co. Inc.

Knickerbocker Bear, 1930s

His design and colour are conventional: less so are his round, tin eyes with their goggling look of surprise!

HEAD Characteristically large, wide, broad-browed and flat-topped.

MUZZLE Long and blunt, shaped to give a quite naturalistic profile. The realistic modelling is achieved by using an inset muzzle cut from a separate piece of fabric, a feature found on many Knickerbocker bears from this period. The mohair of the muzzle is slightly clipped, as usual, for contrast, and is in good condition.

NOSE AND MOUTH Sewn in black thread; nose vertically stitched.

EARS Large, round and slightly cupped, they are set wide apart at the corners of the head and sewn across the facial seams.

ARMS Short, well-shaped, with distinct wrists and an upward curve at the paw. The paws are long and tapering.

PADS Long and narrow with a straight edge at the wrist. The paws are white, to contrast with the dark cinnamon fur, and made of velveteen, Knickerbocker's favourite fabric for paws.

BODY Top quality mohair. The dark cinnamon colour was very popular among American bears at this time, although Knickerbocker often used more unusual shades.

HUMP AND BACK The very straight back ending in a hump at the neck is a typical, though not invariable, Knickerbocker feature.

LEGS Relatively short with short, rounded feet.

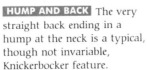

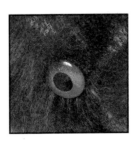

EYES Coloured eyes are not unusual among the Knickerbocker family of bears. In this case they are a speckled browny-green shade, and made of tin, rather than the glass eyes common during this period.

31

KNICKERBOCKER TOY Co. Inc.

ABOVE AND LEFT: A lovely lady from the 1930s has found a hat to match her green glass eyes, but her little embroidered red tongue peeps out as she considers what else to wear. Made of brown mohair plush, she has typical Knickerbocker velveteen pads and an inset muzzle. Her contemporary on the left has beautiful deep gold mohair. Its fine condition makes him a collector's dream, but perhaps also an object of pity, since it betrays that he was never a beloved playmate.

RIGHT: Another fine bear from the 1930s. One of his brown and black glass eyes (possibly replacements for the originals) needs a little surgery, but he has taken commendable care of the woven Knickerbocker label sewn into his chest seam (inset). This company also sometimes stitched the label with its lucky horseshoe logo into the left ear.

Winston

"Winston is a 1930s Knickerbocker bear with a fascinating, history as a lucky charm," Barnaby began his tale of this very unusual bear. "Could he bring me some luck?" asked Junior. "I don't think so," replied Barnaby doubtfully, "but he is responsible for increasing the numbers of children in need of a teddy. In 1946 Winston's owner, the mother of a large family, listened to her daughter's complaint that she still had no children even after six years of marriage. The young woman was instructed to place Winston at the foot of her bed. Within four years, the lady and her husband had been blessed with three children of their own, including a boy called, naturally enough, Winston! In 1966 she passed the bear on to her own daughter, who for three years had failed to conceive. Astoundingly, the magic worked again, and subsequently Winston was lent to other would-be mothers with equal success. He has now taken up a well-earned retirement in a teddy museum – but nowhere near a bed!"

RIGHT: A mere youngster from the 1950s, green-eyed Cheeky Charlie (right) has the typical high quality mohair, large, wide-set ears, broad, flat-topped head and short limbs of the Knickerbocker clan.

AETNA TOY ANIMAL CO.

A Short-lived Trademark

"Next," announced Barnaby, adopting a yogic position to clear his head after all this lecturing, "we come to the Aetna Toy Animal Company of New York, founded in 1901. From 1906 to 1915 they marketed the Aetna Bear – originally known as the Keystone Bear. Aetna Bears, in seven sizes, were of high quality mohair, fully jointed and, as advertisements boasted, artist-designed. In design they are typical early Americans, with the humped back, long limbs, big feet and triangular face we have learned to look for. And happily the company had the sense to use a trademark, an oval ink stamp on the left foot, although in many cases this has faded with the years."

"'Teddy's Bear' was such a hit that the United States saw the creation of a great many teddy bear manufacturers like Aetna in the same period, 1906 to 1907," Barnaby added, "but most of them were short-lived. They did, however, prompt long-established companies like Steiff, in Europe and America, to hone their marketing skills and produce a range of novelty bears."

LEFT: *An Aetna bear from c. 1908 carries his years well. His glass eyes (replacing the boot buttons favoured by his older brothers) are still bright, and his mohair plush and felt pads are in fair condition, although the 'AETNA' logo once stamped on his paw has worn off.*

AETNA TOY ANIMAL Co.

Aetna Bear, c. 1907.

Bears produced by the Aetna Toy Animal Company, such as the well-preserved example shown here, were highly typical of early American design.

HEAD Round with a broad forehead. The long muzzle and triangular face are typical of American bears of this period.

EARS Large, rounded and slightly curved. They are moderately wide-set and positioned high on the head in the face seams.

EYES Traditional black shoe buttons (popular until World War I), set quite close together on the central panel seam.

NOSE Triangular, fitted between the facial seams at the tip of the muzzle. Hand-embroidered with vertical stitches in black floss

BODY Of moderate length, with the traditional slight hump.

ARMS Long and slender, with a slight upward curve at the wrists. The paws are slender, with oval pads in beige felt. Five long black claws are stitched on the plush from the pad seams.

The Aetna Toy Animal Company was unusual among early American bear manufacturers in marking their teddies with an identifying logo – a printed black oval line surrounding the trade name, stamped on the right foot. The trademark was bought in 1919 by E.I. Horsmann Company of New York.

LEGS Long and thin, with pronounced ankles and large feet, again with five black stitched claws. The oval felt pads are reinforced with thin cardboard, forming a flat surface on which the company's identifying logo (not visible on this bear) was stamped.

BRUIN MANUFACTURING Co.

Rare Bears With 'Imported Voices'

"Another short-lived company of the early period," Barnaby continued, "was the Bruin Manufacturing Company of New York. They too set up from 1907 as makers of quality teddies, which they advertised as 'Superior to the Best of Imported Goods'. Like Aetna bears, Bruins are traditionally American in design, with long bodies and limbs. They are fully jointed and made of quality mohair plush, with wood wool stuffing and boot button eyes. Bruin's speciality was its 'imported voices', growler mechanisms imported from Germany." Junior practised growling before asking, "Do they have labels?" "Yes," Barnaby confirmed, "a blue and red woven silk label with the letters 'BMC' in gold thread, stitched on to the foot, though these don't often survive.

BELOW: This Bruin trio answer (from left to right) to the names Awful, Blissful and Wistful. Awful's pads and Blissful's nose are somewhat the worse for wear, but the latter still boasts the rare BMC label on his right foot. The fine condition of the fur of all proves the high quality of mohair used.

BRUIN MANUFACTURING Co.

Bruin Bear, c. 1907

A particularly sweet, melting expression adds something special to the traditional American design.

EYES Brown glass with black pupils, quite small and set fairly close together in the centre panel head seams.

NOSE AND MOUTH The vertically stitched, oblong nose and inverted T mouth are hand-embroidered in a light brown floss to match the blond fur. The fur on the muzzle may have been clipped originally, but has now worn away.

It is particularly pleasing to find a Bruin still displaying the original trademark BMC label, even when, as in this case, it is somewhat battered and faded.

MOHAIR Long and silky, of the high quality associated with the Bruin brand. The soft blond colour sets off the sweet facial expression of this appealing bear.

ARMS Long and tapering, with upcurved paws. The low shoulders are a feature of certain Bruin bears. The three claws are stitched on the plush, in the same light brown floss as is used for the nose and mouth.

LEGS Short, with big, round feet. The pads are beige felt with stitched claws. The right footpad has been repaired with care to retain part of the precious label.

CHARACTER TOY & NOVELTY Co.

Character Studies

"In 1932, the Character Novelty Company in Connecticut was born." Barnaby announced . "People say I'm a real character," said Junior. "Don't fish for compliments," reprimanded Barnaby. "After World War II they hooked on to a winning line in stuffed animals and teddies, traditional and unjointed until they closed down in 1983."

RIGHT AND BELOW RIGHT: Two Character cousins share a family resemblance. The gold mohair trumpet player dates from c. 1948, and his brown buddy in the bow tie from c. 1950-1955. Both have endearing smiles formed by two curved, horizontal stitches, and typical Character eyes: black shoe buttons stitched on to white felt circles.

BELOW AND LEFT: Another pair of characters! The 1920s blond in the big hat has a comically belligerent look. His darker friend sports the metal nose and velveteen pads of the 1920s and retains the luscious colour of his dark cinnamon fur despite a few honourable scars.

CHARACTER TOY & NOVELTY Co.

Character Bear, 1940s

No label, but the Character characteristics are all there!

HEAD Wide and round, with a high forehead and flat top. The short muzzle is made from an inset piece of clipped plush.

EARS Large, flat and wide set, the top edges are sewn into the face seams.

EYES Rich amber glass with painted black pupils.

NOSE A narrow oblong of black vertical stitches.

ARMS AND LEGS Very short and thick. There is no shaping to the solid little legs and blunt feet, but the even shorter arms taper to narrow paws and have a distinct curve at the wrist.

PADS light beige felt of oval or teardrop shape. As with many, though not all, Character bears, there are no claws.

BODY Solid and thick set, with low set arms and slight narrowing at the hips. The mohair is fine quality.

RIGHT: In the period before World War II, teddy bear manufacturers experimented with a range of nose materials including leather, celluloid and even, as here, tin.

ABOVE: Frayed but still flying jauntily, the cloth tag sewn into the left ear seam of another 1940s bear identifies his Character beyond argument.

GUND

Annie Get Your Gund!

"As well as that of the famous cowgirl Annie Oakley, Connecticut was also the birthplace of the Gund Manufacturing Company in 1898," Barnaby went on, "founded in 1898, though the firm moved to New York a few years later. They too began with a range of toys, introducing teddy bears in 1906. When founder Adolph Gund retired in 1925, his assistant Jacob Swedlin (who began life with the firm as a janitor!) bought the company. He expanded into such novelties as mechanical jumping animals and Walt Disney characters, though of course he kept on with the teddies. In the 1950s Gund moved to Brooklyn and produced the Dreamies series, unjointed bears in modern synthetics. In the 1970s they moved to New Jersey and made the break from mass production to up-market collectables like the extra-soft 'Collector's Classics'. The '1983 Anniversary Bear' celebrating their 85th birthday was another winner, followed by special annual bears every year since. In 1991 a new, award-winning line was the limited edition, hand-made Signature Collection. Today the firm is larger than ever, with many of its bears made in the Far East."

BELOW: One of the newest lines in bears, from America's oldest soft toy manufacturer, Gold Dust belongs to the Signature Collection. His laughing face suggests he doesn't take this collecting rage too seriously – but, just in case, his foot is numbered and signed by Gund's director of design, Jacob Swedlin's daughter Rita Swedlin Raiffe.

ABOVE: 'Gotta Getta Gund', runs the firm's slogan, and collectors flock to buy this cuddly trio, representatives of three of Gund's top collectable lines. Sweet Thing, the portly blond on the right, is another of the 1990s Signature Collection. The bear in the middle is the 1993 Gundy bear, eleventh member of a range produced annually since 1983, in limited editions each available only for a single year. On the left, Huggy Bear was born in the purple as a 1992 member of the huggable 'Collector's Classics' range.

GUND

Gund Bear, 1930s

Gund bears of this period whose identity are proven without doubt are hard to find, but this perky little fellow still boasts his original labels.

EYES Large, round 'googly' eyes made of celluloid give a comical stare. The black pupils move freely within the white outer circles, enabling the bear to turn his gaze in different directions.

LIMBS Short and stout, curving at wrist and ankle. The paws are spoon-shaped, the feet round and stubby. The pads are made of beige felt and have no claws. All four limbs are jointed.

EARS Set wide apart, they are large, round and slightly cupped.

HEAD Large and round. The pointed, protruding muzzle of short-pile plush shows signs of wear. The vertically stitched, shield-shaped nose and smiling mouth are sewn in black thread.

MOHAIR His wool plush in the popular cinnamon shade is in commendable condition for his age.

BODY A short round body gives a reasssuringly cuddly appearance. In profile we can see he has the slightly humped back traditional to American bears of this period.

Unknown American Bears

Bears Anonymous

"We've looked at some of the big names among American teddy bear manufacturers," said Barnaby, "now let's look at the bears without names. A great many early American bears have to be classified as 'maker unknown' because few of the early companies went in for labels, and, just to make things harder, the boom years of the early 1900s saw a great many short-lived firms come and go. They included the American Doll and Toy Manufacturing Company, Art Novelty Company, Columbia Teddy Bear Manufacturers, Hecla, Harman Manufacturing of New York, Miller Manufacturing Company, Strauss Manufacturing Company..." "Stop, stop!" cried Junior. "Enough's enough! But how are these poor bears supposed to keep any sense of identity if they don't know their makers?" "It's not as bad as all that," Barnaby reassured him. "While there is considerable variety among American bears, most of them do have the distinctive American look. They may be in the style popularized by Ideal, with triangular face, big ears, and narrow body; or the other traditional style with round head, short muzzle, long body, straight limbs and small feet." "I'll never remember all that," groaned poor Junior. "Never mind, said Barnaby. "In any case, 'a bear's a bear for all that' and true bear-lovers will value them anyway." "What's in a name?" countered the irrepressible youngster.

BELOW RIGHT: Atten-shun! Three Bandsmen Bears by two unidentified, 1920s-1930s manufacturers, deserve commendation for preserving their parade uniforms so conscientiously.

LEFT. Advertisers quickly spotted the teddy bear's publicity potential. This little bear was a giveaway with Women's Home Journal in the 1920s.

LEFT: Two more members of Bears Anonymous have joined forces. The little lad in dungarees, from 1906-1907, is typical of his period. The red bear – an unusual colour – is an Electric Eyes Bear with battery-operated flashing eyes. Several companies introduced these bears, but the easily broken mechanism soon outweighed the novelty value, and few survive.

UNKNOWN AME

LEFT: A long body and round head show that Brutus, 1920s-1930s, is a Yankee. He is made of deep purple plush.

RIGHT: In contrast, the train-loving ted, from 1908, has the equally American-style triangular head popularized by Ideal.

FAR LEFT: His date is unknown, but he is a good example of a typical early American bear, with the rather stern inverted Y mouth common among his kin.

LEFT: No stern looks here, but an early bear whose smile has outlasted much of his stuffing, perhaps cheered by the kindness of the person who darned his paws and put new furry pads on his feet.

RIGHT: Two bears to test the collector's knowledge! Momma Bear has a narrower head and more pointed muzzle than the typical American bear, but her long body and relatively short, straight limbs help to identify her birthplace. However, her adopted son, also American, is different again, plumper in the body and longer in the limbs.

Eddie

Eddie isn't fooling when he harks back to the "follies" of his youth, for his first human friend, vaudeville star Marilyn Miller, is best known as a member of the famous Ziegfeld Follies! Way back in 1904, Marilyn was taking a break from the vaudeville circuit, where she toured with the Five Columbians, to spend the summer with her family in Findlay, Ohio. She took the opportunity to present her young neighbour Eddie Paige with this handsome cinnamon mohair bear. Eddie the bear remained in the Paige family for 81 years before retiring to the Carrousel Museum, Michigan, where he regales fellow inmates with stories of the past. Though his mohair is torn in places, his felt pads are, astonishingly, in mint condition, and his black shoe-button eyes retain all the sparkle of an honorary vaudeville star.

RIGHT AND BELOW: Three more – well, two and a bit – anonymous but lovingly preserved early Americans show the wide variety of size and style. The characteristic long body is particularly well displayed by the tall gent in the red bow tie.

Rocking In Retirement

Cleaned and repaired in the teddy bear museum, this little bear came direct from the original owner, who was two years old when her parents bought it in a Michigan General Store in 1912.

UNKNOWN AMERICAN BEARS

ABOVE : A cute quartet whose history may be a blank, but who display a range of lively personalities. We have (from left to right) a donnish type from c. 1920, a wistful lassie of unknown date, a light-footed lad from c. 1908, and, behind one of the world's larger bow ties, a well-preserved chap who may be the oldest of the group, thought to date from 1906.

Second Hand Rose

Two young antique dealers who specialize in vintage clothing made the find of a lifetime while exploring the attic of a Victorian mansion in Michigan. All manner of objects had been lovingly stored in the attic for almost a century, and as the young couple worked through the strata they came across what amounted to a series of time capsules for each decade. At last they reached an old steamer trunk containing goods from the turn of the century. Among the treasures inside was an old shoebox, and they lifted its lid to find this wonderful bear. Deep in her unsuspected hiding place she had preserved her youth, and was in mint condition. Her blond mohair was as bright as new, and even her squeaker still worked, though very faintly – hardly surprisingly after her long years of silence. Her finders rushed with their discovery to the Carrousel Museum, where she acquired her fur neckpiece, felt hat with ribbons and feathers, tiny red leather purse and – at last – a name: Second Hand Rose.

AMERICAN FAMILY TREE

Westward Ho!

1907

Advertised as a 'self-whistling bear' in 1907, Luther was known for his cheery tunes.

"The family album of our kin in the States," said Barnaby, "is in itself a history of the teddy bear from the time we landed here." "Did we land in Arkansas?" asked Junior. "They once called that the 'Bear State'." "No, nor under California's 'Bear Flag', but in New York," replied Barnaby, "from where we have colonized the nation 'from sea to shining sea', as did its founders!" This highfalutin' talk was a little over Junior's head, so he turned to the album.

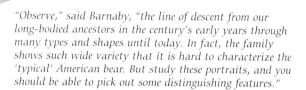

"Observe," said Barnaby, "the line of descent from our long-bodied ancestors in the century's early years through many types and shapes until today. In fact, the family shows such wide variety that it is hard to characterize the 'typical' American bear. But study these portraits, and you should be able to pick out some distinguishing features."

c. 1915

Like his hero 'Teddy' Roosevelt, Wilbur was an all-round action fellow.

1920s

A price on his head of 25 cents gave Two Bit Daniley, from Pennsylvania, his unusual name.

1950s

Chuck delighted his proud mother when he won first prize for most loveable bear.

1950s

Wounded many times in action and even decorated for bravery, Arthur has now retired.

1970s

Mom and Mickey pose for the charming portrait that Dad carried everywhere in his wallet.

1980s

Benjy is sure he will one day make the grade and play for his favourite team, the Dodgers.

c. 1910

Max, a traditional type devoted to his family, ruled the roost in 1910-1914.

c. 1910

Loretta chose a tasteful cerise ribbon to set off her dark blonde mohair.

c. 1912

Aunt Eunice donned her favourite lace cape to pose for her portrait.

1920s

His New Yorker cousin Augustus preferred to stick with a more sophisticated lifestyle.

1930s

Sweet little Southern gal Caresse had beaux riding from miles around in the 1930s.

1935

Swing music was Minocqua's thing, though only when nobody was watching.

1944

Voted 'Bear With the Most Character', Just Ted was neverthelesss still popular with ordinary folk.

1980

Mischka travelled to the Moscow Olympics in 1980 - as mascot for the games.

1985

Joe joined up to make a career in the armed forces, but never forgot to write home.

1992

Daisy wears flowers in her hair, celebrating fashion's revival of the 1960s.

1992

Justin looks forward to a successful future for himself and his descendents.

· *Bear Tales* ·

WARTIME BEARS

Bears Of War

"Let us now sing famous bears," proclaimed Barnaby, "and in particular, ursine war heroes." "I thought all bears would be conscientious objectors," objected Junior. "The Bear Scouts' Code says we have to be peaceable, reliable and faithful. It doesn't say anything about fighting!" "Ah," said Barnaby, "but it's understood that a bear will always stand by his owner. When owners went to war, naturally their bears went too, and many a soldier, sailor or airman was heartened by the presence of one true friend. Bear mascots travelled on dangerous missions, or even served in prisoner-of-war camps; and they also served who only stayed behind to comfort loved ones at home, bearing the brunt of bombing, evacuation and dreaded telegrams."

LEFT AND BELOW: Teddies comforted frightened children in wartime. To evacuees sent away from home to escape the bombs, a teddy might be the only friend left. And a cheery ted fixed to a gas mask case made the compulsory gas mask less alarming for little ones.

· *Theodore Bear* ·

Theodore wears his battered mohair with pride, for his are heroic scars. A much-loved companion since 1907, he faced out World War II with his owner. From 1940 they shared four years in a German prisoner-of-war camp, then survived RAF strafing of the train taking them home. After the war Theodore spent seven years aiding his owner's relief work in displaced persons' camps. In 1988 the battered bear was auctioned for the charity Research into Ageing, and found a peaceful retirement home.

WARTIME BEARS

• Kermit Bear •

A mohair doughboy! Wartime bears were often dressed up patriotically in uniform. Kermit (below), a 1916 American bear, wears 'doughboy' uniform, complete with sturdy boots, and an impressive array of medals. His threadbear state suggests that he saw active service, in the field or on the home front.

• Fritz Bear •

After World War II, Fritz was found under a Nissen hut floor, where a German prisoner of war had hidden him. Despite his battered and dusty state, he was clearly a bear of some status, for his knitted jacket bore a 1939 German War Merit Cross, with a British Royal Army Ordnance Corps cap badge and a collection of embroidered military insignia. When spruced up, he proved to boast a good family name as well, for he was identified as a 1906 Steiff.

RIGHT: *A World War II air raid warden found this little bear in the ruins of a London home hit by a doodlebug. She'd lost both ears, an eye, and her name, but he took her home. Some home surgery (including ears made from old sock toes) improved her looks, and a name was easy: she now answers to Blitz!*

· Bear Tales ·

SEA-FARING BEARS

Jolly Jack Bear

"Oh, a life on the ocean wave!" sang Barnaby. Junior raised an eyebrow. "I thought boat trips always made you sick?" he said. "Yes, well, it isn't my fault if the sea's always so uppy and downy," Barnaby replied. "But when I think of mariner bears, a strong paw on the helm and all that sort of thing, it stirs the blood, you know." "Stick to the seaside deckchair," Junior said firmly.

"Telescope, compass, navigation manual... we're all set to be deckchair sailors!"

· Captain Arthur Crown ·

Too much swashbuckling left this bear bald, one-eyed and with the stuffing quite knocked out of him. But after surgery he emerged with a piratical eyepatch and distinctly nautical swagger – and a new name: Captain Arthur Crown ("'alf a crown' – the price he fetched in his battered state).

SEA-FARING BEARS

• Martin •

And here on the left we have Able Seaman Martin to represent the lower decks. This sturdy mariner is a bit portly these days to dance the hornpipe. But his "bearitone" voice cheers his shipmates as he runs through his wide repertoire of sea songs, from shanties like "Blow the bear down" to ballads of bold Admiral Bruin. Today his snowy shirt and spotless kitbag suggest he's off ashore to see his sweetheart.

• Jack •

Captain Crown's great rival is Jack the Bear, on the right, an honest sea-bear who not unnaturally resents the Captain's smart uniform ("found in a dressing-up box!" sneers Jack) and raffish air. It's quite clear to him that the piratical bruin deserves a long walk down a short plank and a period marooned on Treasureless Island without any honey for tea. But the best-laid plans of mice and bears can be brought to nothing by quite little snags...like the fact that Jack's sea legs aren't too good, and in fact a quick survey of the duck pond is about his limit to date!

GERMAN TEDDY BEARS

❤

It Started With Steiff

"Teddy Roosevelt may have been the spiritual father of the teddy bear," Barnaby remarked "but Germany, rather than the United States, is our true Motherland." "I don't see how that can be," Junior interrupted. "Bear with me," Barnaby beamed. "Long before Roosevelt's bear cub caught the fancy of the American public, Germany already had a name for manufacturing soft toys, including realistic bears. Many of these were push-alongs on wheels, or mechanicals – often poor quality, so few survive today. At around the time the first 'Teddy's Bears' appeared in American stores, a German seamstress called Margarete Steiff began producing jointed bears of teddy rather than naturalistic type, prompted by her nephew, Richard Steiff, who had used his drawings of bears at the local zoo to make a prototype of a bear-doll. In 1904 the toy trade discovered Steiff bears and hundreds of thousands were ordered for export to America." "A case of Ready, Teddy, Go!" cried Junior. Barnaby suppressed a shudder, but had to agree. "It was indeed. Other German firms, such as Bing, Hermann and Schuco, were quick to jump on the bear-wagon, but Steiff didn't need to stifle the competition. During the 'bear years' of 1903-1908 public demand for teddies was insatiable. Today these early German bears, particularly Steiffs, are a collector's dream, especially since they are better documented than their American cousins."

FAR LEFT: German manufacturers always loved novelty bears. From the 1920s, this is a most unusual Jack-in-the-box teddy.

LEFT: The 1920 clockwork clown bear with bell and stick was made by Moses Kohnsturm of Furth.

RIGHT: A popular colour in Germany in the 1930s, brown-tipped blond mohair tended to fade with age.

ABOVE RIGHT: Teddy bear postcards are very collectable.

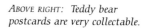

GERMAN TEDDY BEARS

EARS Large, high set, and with an unusual, rather dog-like forward tilt.

German Bear, 1920s

An early bear from the 1920s by an unknown German manufacturer. Positive identification of this handsome bruin is impossible in the absence of any tag or label, but he retains his nationality. The design is unmistakably Germanic.

EYES Not the round black bootbuttons of earlier German bears, but the glass eyes which came into favour from the early 1920s.

NOSE AND MOUTH Embroidered in brown thread. The nose is worked in vertical stitches; the mouth is a single long horizontal stitch caught up into an inverted Y.

HEAD The wide, round head and naturalistic, long muzzle (less pointed than a Steiff bear's) are clear pointers to a German manufacturer despite the absence of any identifying label.

ARMS The very long arms with their upward curve at the wrists demonstrate another typical characteristic of German bear style.

LEGS Also long, and tapering towards very large feet with felt pads, where the remains of brown, stitched claws can just be seen.

FUR A rather smart green-tipped mohair, retaining much of its texture but little of its original, sadly impermanent dye.

GERMAN TEDDY BEARS

ORIGINAL KOCH

LEFT AND RIGHT: These two playmates are certainly having a ball! The shaggy bouncer on the left is known to have been made by the Koch company, which produced teddies in the 1950s, but his anonymous companion bears no clue to his maker. Both have the distinctive long muzzle of German bears, particularly marked in the clean-shaven Koch character.

TOP RIGHT: Identity tags can be fun. The Koch (German 'cook') tag has a bear in a chef's hat, holding a spoon.

CENTRE: The logo for the Anker company is a punning anchor and a lion.

GERMAN TEDDY BEARS

BELOW: This 1970 Steiff Zotty bear is proud to be German, stepping out in his national costume of lederhosen and Tyrolean hat with jaunty feather.

Bare Years, Then A Bear Revival

Two World Wars proved a setback for Germany's production and export of bears. Some manufacturers, including Steiff, stopped making bears altogether in the early 1940s and turned over their factories to munitions work. Others, like Steiff's long-established rival Gebrüder Hermann, kept going only by moving to the US Zone in West Germany. But you can't keep a good bear down, and by the 1950s Germany's teddy trade was in full swing again. The Steiff company quickly won back its position as bear leader, but other firms re-established their grip and new companies sprang into being. In the 1970s, cheap imports from East Asia provided worrying competition, but this was only a 'paws' for thought. Almost immediately came a new impetus for growth as teddies expanded their territory from the world of children's toys into that of expensive collectables, and manufacturers in Germany as elsewhere took the hint. By the early 1980s both Steiff and Hermann were producing limited-edition replicas of their early products, as well as a number of anniversary bears. Many of these are designed for the American market. Bear collecting in Germany today focuses on antique rather than artists' bears, and especially on Steiff bears. In 1986, collector Florentine Wagner founded Berlin's teddy bear museum, which boasts more than 2,000 residents.

BELOW LEFT: The Roaring Twenties ride again! Anyone less likely to roar than dainty Teddy Rose is hard to imagine, but she is in fact a 1992 replica of a 1925 Steiff original.

BELOW RIGHT: Happy is the real thing from 1926. She wears her years lightly, and the collector who paid £55,000 (US $86,000) for her at Sotheby's in 1989 will have valued her sweet expression as highly as the lovely condition of her tipped mohair.

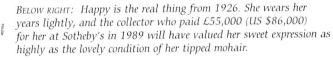

Zotty Bears

A Shaggy Bear Story

In 1951, Steiff invented the Zotty bear, a chubby chappie characterized by his open mouth and the unique long-hair mohair which gives him his name." "Zottig must be German for shaggy," said Junior. "That's right," went on Barnaby. "His permanent grin is highlighted with a peach-coloured felt lining and felt or painted tongue, while his fur has a delightful two-tone effect, created by using pile of a different shade from the backing fabric. An instant hit, he was copied by Hermann and other German firms, though you can always tell a Steiff Zotty, even if his identifying button has gone astray, by his contrast-coloured chest panel. Zotties come in a range of sizes and colours, and include a Sleeping Zotty made by Steiff in a lying-down pose, 1960s dressed Zotties in felt rompers or little jackets, and Steiff's Minky Zotty of 1975 in a luxurious synthetic plush designed to resemble mink."

RIGHT: A Zotty forebear! He isn't particularly shaggy, but this 1945 Hermann bear has the open mouth with felt lining and red felt tongue that six years later Steiff adopted to create the Zotty.

BELOW: Peach-coloured chest panels identify the 1950s family as Steiff Zotties. The rest of their fur is given its subtle shading by the use of shaggy blond mohair plush on a dark brown, woven base fabric.

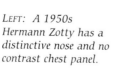

LEFT: A 1950s Hermann Zotty has a distinctive nose and no contrast chest panel.

Peter Bear

All The Better To Eat You With...

"Most early bears are rare because young owners loved them to pieces. But Gebrüder Sussenguth's 1925 Peter Bear is scarce simply because he wasn't loved." "Those long teeth, rolling eyes and waggling tongue are a bit frightening," said Junior. "That's exactly what the children he was meant to charm felt, and so very few were sold. But more recently, his eccentric grin (as well as his rarity) won the heart of collectors, who were ecstatic when, in 1976, a hundred mint-condition Peters were found abandoned in a shut-down East German factory and smuggled out to the West."

ABOVE: 'Bär wie lebend' boasts the label on Peter's box: 'Bear most natural-like finish'. Too life-like for some!

LEFT AND ABOVE: Peter was made in beige tipped with dark brown, dark grey tipped with white or, rarest of all, gold plush. To modern eyes he has a slightly manic charm, but his rolling eyes and realistic, moulded teeth spelled market disaster.

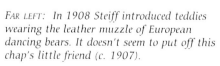

STEIFF

They Bear Their Name With Pride

"It's hard to imagine," remarked Barnaby, "that when Richard Steiff invented his new doll-like bear toy, it wasn't immediately spotted as a winner. In fact, Margarete Steiff, doyenne of the Steiff company, was unenthusiastic." "Goodness," cried Junior. "It doesn't bear thinking of!" "But all was well," Barnaby went on. "Richard was lucky in his timing. His bear proved a smash hit at the 1903 Leipzig Toy Fair because of the United States' love affair with Roosevelt's bear cub. After that, of course, the teddy won its place not as a political icon but on its own merits as a cuddly toy blending the virtues of doll and stuffed animal. Steiff remained the most prominent teddy bear manufacturer through sheer dedication. Quality remained a constant, but in every other way Richard Steiff and his successors experimented and expanded. Even the unavailability of traditional materials in the inter-war years couldn't stop Steiff. Bears continued to roll off the production line in a fabric made from reconstituted nettles! Richard Steiff's brother Hugo brought his engineering skills into play, introducing clockwork bears. Other novelties included roly poly bears, nodding bears with a cute little tail to operate the mechanism, a hot-water bottle ted and, later, dressed bears like Nimrod the hunter, complete with wooden rifle. Over the years Steiff brought endless expertise and ingenuity to bear upon maintaining their reputation as leader of the bear pack."

TOP LEFT: Margarete Steiff, a victim of polio, worked among her employees in her wheelchair.

BELOW RIGHT: In this family group, a 1950s youngster hogs the chair while his elderly relations (c. 1910) have to make do with the floor.

CENTRE LEFT: Here we have two novelties. The 1908 Roly Poly bear is quite legless, but keeps his balance with a weighted base. His royal friend is an extremely rare Steiff skittle of velvet and wood, from a set of ten made c. 1895.

FAR LEFT: In 1908 Steiff introduced teddies wearing the leather muzzle of European dancing bears. It doesn't seem to put off this chap's little friend (c. 1907).

LEFT: This Clown Bear, c. 1927 is a rarer bear. He has lost his original ruff.

STEIFF

Steiff Bear, c. 1910

A highly desirable classic early Steiff of c. 1910 in excellent condition.

HEAD Not as large as many other makers', with rounded back and the traditional protruding muzzle, its length emphasized by close clipping of the mohair.

EYES Small, black, wooden boot buttons, set just outside the face seams – an identifying factor of Steiff bears, for many manufacturers set the eyes into these seams.

NOSE The hand-embroidered nose is vertically stitched, always the case with early small Steiffs like this one (bigger bears had horizontally stitched noses).

BODY Long, with a slightly smaller hump than that of his predecessors. He is made in good quality short-pile gold mohair and stuffed with wood wool.

ARMS Very long – in fact, when the bear is standing, they reach his knees! They taper from the shoulder and curve at the wrist.

LEGS Quite long, tapering towards pronounced ankles.

FEET Like those of all early Steiffs, they are very large, measuring in length a fifth of the bear's body height!

PADS Long and narrow, made of beige felt. The well-preserved, straight claws are embroidered in black thread across the mohair plush, four claws on both paws and feet.

ABOVE: The Steiff 'Button in Ear' trademark was introduced in 1904. Originally it bore an embossed elephant.

CENTRE LEFT AND RIGHT, FAR RIGHT: In 1905 Steiff patented its button, and dropped the elephant in favour of the simple name STEIFF in block capitals, or, later, cursive script, still in use today (far right). Other manufacturers were prompt to adopt the ear button, but Steiff took legal action to make their rivals drop the button or move it to the body or arm. From 1908–1909 a cloth label was added, and from 1926 a paper label on the chest, which hardly ever survives today.

STEIFF

"I'm going to be a tumbling bear when I grow up," announced Junior. "But remember, pride goes before a fall," Barnaby cautioned him.

ABOVE AND BELOW FAR LEFT: The very long "bear-faced" muzzle of the rare 1903 Steiff contrasts with the more teddy-like features of his 1906 cousin.

ABOVE: Two golden oldies from c. 1905. The little bear is one of the rare rod-jointed bears, which were only in production for one year. His unusual nose, made of moulded sealing-wax, gives the game away: such noses are only found on rod-jointed Steiffs.

Casing The Joints

"To appreciate Steiff's perfectionist approach," Barnaby went on, "let's consider jointing. Their first bear had very simple joints made of string." "You're stringing me along!" cried Junior. "Not at all. But Richard Steiff wasn't satisfied. These joints let him market his bear as 'Beweglich,' (movable) – but string breaks. Next, in 1905, he came up with straight metal rods running through the body. These rod-jointed bears are now very rare. Double wire jointing came next, followed in 1905 by disc-jointing (card discs held in place with a metal pin), which Steiff have used ever since." "This technical stuff bores me 'Steiff'," muttered Junior. "Maybe, but you need disc joints if you want to go disco dancing," Barnaby pointed out.

The Centre Seam Bear

'Centre-seam' bears are rare and much valued – but they were designed not to delight collectors, but merely as a Steiff economy measure to save on expensive fabric. Six complete teddy heads could be cut from each length of mohair plush – with a bit left over. Rather than waste the remnant, it was used for a seventh bear with its central face gusset cut in two pieces rather than one. So one bear in every seven boasted a centre seam running from the tip of the nose to the back of the head. Of course, on a smart new teddy the seam would be well-covered by mohair, but balding pates like that of elderly Albert on the left reveal all.

BELOW: Two centre-seams from 1905, Bo on the left and Dearheart have clearly had an easier life.

LEFT: Poor Albert went to pieces when he was dumped in a cellar. Lovingly restored, he rewarded his finders when he proved to be no common bear but a rare centre-seam of c. 1910.

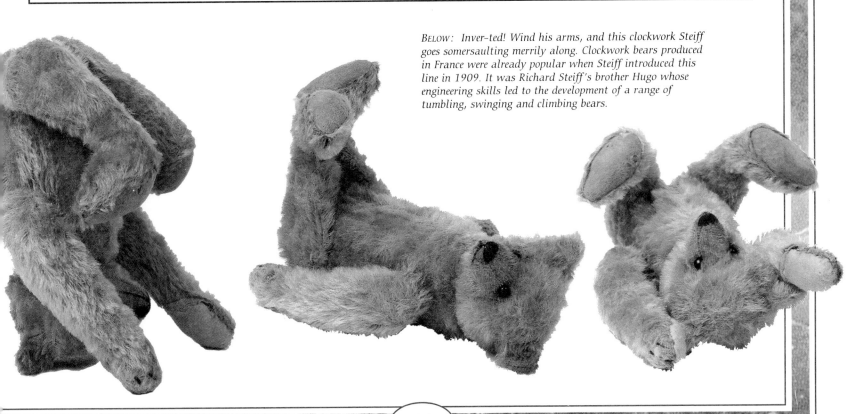

BELOW: Inver-ted! Wind his arms, and this clockwork Steiff goes somersaulting merrily along. Clockwork bears produced in France were already popular when Steiff introduced this line in 1909. It was Richard Steiff's brother Hugo whose engineering skills led to the development of a range of tumbling, swinging and climbing bears.

STEIFF

LEFT: *Real bears come in a range of colours from black through many shades of brown to white. As far as Steiff teddies are concerned, the sky's the limit and the range runs through the rainbow. But the colour that has come to be seen as standard is a rich gold, as worn by this pre-1910 bear with his beautiful long, curly mohair.*

ABOVE CENTRE: *Collectors covet rare white and cinnamon bears. Ulysses, from the early 1920s, is keeping his valued ear button under his hat, but proudly displays his white mohair.*

ABOVE RIGHT: *The lovely rich cinnamon shade is seen on The Old Man, pre-1911, who takes his name from the owner who loved him.*

RIGHT: *A soft honey colour was chosen for Ricky, made c. 1906-1907. Even this early, Steiff was changing from the original long-nosed 'animal' look in favour of a cuddlier, short-faced teddy.*

FAR RIGHT: *His sooty friend is a real rarity. Steiff only made 494 black bears, perhaps because black fails to set off the features.*

STEIFF

Donna And Dottty

When two elderly twin sisters sold their Steiff teddy bears to a dealer, there was a risk that the bears might be parted after spending their lives together. Happily, they have been able to move into sheltered accommodation together at the Carrousel Teddy Bear Museum, where they are known as Donna and Dotty, the Dowager Twins.

ABOVE: Donna and Dotty show a close sisterly resemblance, in shape, size (10in/25.4cm) and bright little shoe-button eyes. It is always useful to be able to tell twins apart, and with these two colour is the key. One is white mohair with brown stitched nose and claws, the other brown with black stitching. Or perhaps we should say they were. Years of hugging wore away their mohair, and both were shivering until their new hosts provided crocheted sweaters to keep them warm.

Wilhelm

Wilhelm's haughty carriage is understandable, considering his royal connections. His owner, Max, was a trusted retainer of the German Emperor Wilhelm. In 1918, when the emperor abdicated, Wilhelm helped escort him to Holland. There he and Max settled until Max was killed in World War II, when Max's son took him to safety in England.

Blanche

Blanche's ladylike air belies an adventurous history. Made in 1926, she belonged to a woman who worked in Intelligence as a spy during World War II. Blanche was her trusted companion on her travels. Having acquired a taste for globe-trotting, Blanche was delighted to continue travelling after the war when her owner became an international correspondent.

STEIFF

The Steiff Bear Adap-ted...

"It's wonderful how great traditions go on unchanged," mused Junior, "like Christmas trees, and Steiff bears." "Unchanged?" cried Barnaby. "I don't know about Christmas trees, but Steiff wouldn't be where they are now if they'd tried to stifle change! Bears have to move with the times, like anyone else. Some adaptations were due to outside pressures, like the voiceless bears produced in 1949 when demand outstripped the company's supply of growlers!" "Gosh, I'd hate that!" said Junior. "In some bears, it might be an improvement," said Barnaby. "Steiff also had to respond to changing fashions. In 1950 Swiss buyers wanted bears with shorter arms and bigger heads. Steiff acted promptly – and profitably – to remodel their lines as required."

LEFT: The quality of manufacture remains up to Steiff standards, but this 1950 bear is made of cotton-rayon fabric. Steiff had to resort to this substitute for the traditional mohair because of material shortages after World War II. Post-war regulations also restricted Steiff to manufacturing limited numbers, which until 1947 were for export only.

BELOW: A stern-looking bear from the 1955–1962 period displays one tradition that Steiff have maintained unbroken, the trademark ear button. By his era, mohair was back on the market and, like so many of his forebears, he is resplendent in rich brown mohair plush.

STEIFF

...And The Steiff Bear Perfec-ted!

"The next major setback for Steiff, and other bear-makers," Barnaby went on, "came in the 1970s. Falling birthrates cut the market, and cheap Asian imports brought competition. Steiff tried out cheaper toys without success. But by the end of the decade the Great Bear Revival allowed them to go the other way – producing more expensive super-bears."

LEFT: A 1950 model shows that Steiff had now fully adapted the classic teddy style. Compared with earlier bears, he has shorter limbs, squarer paws, a minimal hump, rounder head and much reduced muzzle.

RIGHT: Modern times: Steiff's 1992 musical bear plays – what else? – 'The Teddy Bears' Picnic'. With big brown eyes and painted eyelashes, set in a heart-shaped face, he has come a long way from more realistic early bears.

BELOW LEFT AND RIGHT: The wheel came full circle in the 1980s, when Steiff turned to their archives to offer replicas of their precious early bears. Dicky (below left) is a 1985 replica of a 1930 beaming bear with decorative painted pads. Baby-Bear on wheels, with bells on his paws, is a 1989 copy of a 1939 pull-along.

GEBRÜDER HERMANN

"Look," cried Junior, "thank goodness our younger Hermann cousins have tags! At least I shall be able to recognize them."

Hurray For Hermann!

"This looks like another important family," said Junior. "Yes, indeed," Barnaby told him. "These are the Hermann bears, another German clan with a long and glorious history. It all began in 1907, at Johann Hermann's toy factory in Sonnenberg. Johann had the forethought to produce not only splendid bears, but a family of his own to continue the tradition, which has now run through three generations and four separate firms, founded by different branches of the Hermann family. After World War II, to avoid the communist regime, Johann's son Bernhard moved the factory to Hirschaid, in the American Zone of Germany, and it was here that the firm of Gebrüder Hermann established itself as a great name in the bear business. It was truly a family business. Bernhard, his wife Ida and their four sons (one of whom died young) built up the reputation of their bears, and today Bernhard's granddaughters maintain the tradition. Early Hermann bears closely resemble their Steiff cousins – in fact, because they only bore a tie-on paper tag which was easily lost, it can be hard to tell whether some of our older relations are Steiffs or Hermanns.

Though since both are much sought after, the lack of a label doesn't really matter to these classic bears!" "Their quality bears out their pedigree, in fact," agreed Junior.

FAR LEFT AND CENTRE: A 1930s bear in gold mohair has the rounded, inset muzzle typical of this firm. His long-suffering pads contrast with those of his 1940s cousin in the hat, who has taken care of both fur and felt!

LEFT: Two Hermanns from the 1950s, one a Zotty, have gone even further and preserved rare original metal swing tags.

BE HA
QUALITY
GERMANY

1911-1929

GEBRÜDER HERMANN

Hermann Bear, 1930s

A splendid example of a Hermann bear sits apparently lost in meditation, dreaming of times (and tags) long past.

MUZZLE Like that of his Steiff relatives, long and pointed, though direct comparison shows it to be slightly shorter and more rounded than a Steiff. A useful distinguishing feature is that Hermanns often have inset muzzles of a different fabric, which may contrast strikingly with the material used for the rest of the bear.

NOSE AND MOUTH Embroidered in black thread. The nose is triangular and horizontally stitched, the mouth the traditional inverted V, slightly curved in a tentative half-smile.

EARS Small, semi-circular, and cut from two pieces: tipped mohair For the back and short-pile or clipped mohair at the front.

ABOVE: A close family resemblance, as the 1930s bear poses on the right with his big brother from c. 1925.
ABOVE CENTRE: The Hermann tag as it appears today.

ARMS AND LEGS Relatively short, with less curve at the paw and smaller feet than earlier bears.

PADS Oval in shape, made of cream felt. The three claws stitched across the pads are a feature common to Hermann bears.

BODY Chunky, with pronounced hump. Common to Hermann bears is the absence of side seams: instead we find a central body seam at back and front.

1930-1939   **1940-1951**   **1952-on**

Hermann's swing tag labels were not meant to be permanent and rarely survive. As we see from this line-up, the 'Teddy' label, like the firm's reputation for quality, has changed very little over the years.

FUR Tipped mohair plush, beige with cinnamon tipping, gives a subtle two-tone effect, somewhat worn away over much of this bear. The short-pile plush of the muzzle is in a contrasting warm cream shade.

"School? No, thank you!" cried Junior. "I think I'll stick to history lessons as provided by my dear uncle Barnaby! Much more fun!"

Above: It's lesson time at the Nostalgic Bear School for six little bears and their teacher. This enchanting mini-class is a limited edition made for the firm's 75th anniversary.

Right: Thoroughly modern Max? Well, not quite. Max is a 1992 bear, but made to a 1930s design. In distressed mohair with suedette pads, and complete with growler, he was made in a limited edition of 500.

Far right: Max's brunette friend was also made in 1992, but to a modern design, though he retains the characteristic family features of tipped mohair, rounded muzzle and long, well-defined limbs.

GEBRÜDER HERMANN

Moving With The Times

Hermann bears have responded with enthusiasm to the modern demand for collectables. Since the early 1980s they have produced a range of limited edition bears: new designs commissioned from American bear artists, an Anniversary Bear to mark the firm's 75th birthday in 1982, and replica bears painstakingly reconstructed from the archives. Hermann's Nostalgic Bears have mohair plush, wood wool stuffing and hand-sewn noses just like their ancestors.

LEFT: A real oldster this time, whose sheepskin coat reminds us of the 1940 mohair shortage.

SCHREYER & CO. (SCHUCO)

Shake Hands – Or Heads – With Schuco

"Take your sticky nose out of that honey, Junior," ordered Barnaby. "If you want amusement, come this way to meet the Schuco family, a fine troupe of entertainers. The Schuco story began in 1912, when Heinrich Müller and Heinrich Schreyer founded Schreyer & Company to make mechanical toys. Müller had worked for Gebrüder Bing, so it was not surprising that the new firm soon started making bears, marketed as Schuco bears, from the firm's initial letters. They had great success with clockwork bears which you wound up with a key to make them march, tumble or play football. These keys were easily lost, though, so a Schuco bear who has kept his holds the key to a fortune! They are also very attractive bears, with dainty, Bing-like features, though Schuco non-mechanical teddies are quite different, with wider heads, bigger eyes and ears, and longer mohair. The famous patented Yes/No bear, introduced in 1921, nods or shakes his head, all done by manipulating the tail, which act as a lever operating the head. From skating bears with wheels to later two-faced bears with exchangeable heads, Schuco bears are highly collectable."

LEFT: Two peckish performers, when wound up, march along licking their lollies.

RIGHT: A rare Schuco Yes/No Bellhop Bear, in integral uniform, still boasts red pillbox hat, leather bag, and even his paper tag.

SC&CO. (SCHUCO)

Schuco Bear, 1950s

A rare Schuco musical Yes/No bear from the 1950s. The sweet facial expression and appealing downward-bent paws make collectors rate such post-war Yes/No bears even more than their older relations.

HEAD Broad, tilted slightly backwards. The dainty pointed muzzle, ears set far back on the head and wide-set eyes go to create an appealing look of child-like innocence and curiosity.

NOSE The nose is moulded black plastic, but the mouth a more traditional inverted T stitched in black thread.

EYES Large, round glass eyes, amber with black pupils, are positioned on the central face seams.

BODY Plump and cuddly, with much reduced hump. The wind-up key on his chest operates an internal Swiss musical box.

RIGHT: Tails I win! Our hero wouldn't dream of looking down on his tiny cousin for, like him, this 1930s miniature is a Yes/No bear with the famous tail mechanism.

ARMS Shorter than on earlier bears, with an appealing begging gesture created by the characteristic downward curve which Schuco favoured. The broad paws have beige felt pads and four claws stitched in black thread across the plush.

LEGS Fairly short and chubby, with big feet. The felt of the footpads is reinforced with an inner lining of stiff card, allowing the bear to stand up sturdily.

TAIL The stumpy little tail is a lever operating an interior metal rod up to the neck joint. When manipulated, it allows the bear to nod, shake his head or turn it from side to side.

SCHREYER & CO. (SCHUCO)

Bears For All Seasons

"Whatever are you doing?" Barnaby asked as Junior rummaged through his suitcase. "I'm looking for some props, so I can pretend to be a Schuco performing bear and join the show!" Junior explained. "I'm afraid without the mechanism, you'd only be a shadow of a Schuco performer," Barnaby told him. "But don't worry. Not all Schucos rely on doing tricks for their appeal. Plenty are just simple honest bears like us."

BELOW LEFT AND RIGHT: *Non-mechanical Schucos like this 1930s cinnamon bear and 1940s bright gold ted have wide heads, big eyes and ears, and long mohair.*

BELOW CENTRE: *Compare the daintier features and shorter fur of mechanicals like the Yes/No brothers.*

BELOW RIGHT: *A lovely 1940s model in splendid condition. Characteristics to look out for in Schucos of this period include large ears, inset muzzle, clear glass eyes, shaven mohair on both muzzle and paws, and a nose style which recalls that of Bing bears, vertically sewn with a longer stitch at each end.*

SCHREYER & CO. (SCHUCO)

BELOW: 1950s models display fluctuating fashions in noses. Despite wear and tear, the lefthand bear's nose still displays vertical stitching, with long end stitches. The middle bear's nose, also vertically sewn, is triangular, while the righthand bear's has horizontal stitches.

LEFT AND FAR LEFT: In the early 1950s, the Yes/No bears were marketed as Tricky bears – the egg-collector still has his medallion with his name on. His schoolboy pal has a cloth body under his clothes, an economy measure at a time when mohair was scarce.

RIGHT: Not a mechanical bear, but the two-tone ted tinkering with his car is evidently mechanically-minded! This 1950s bear with smallish ears and shoe-button eyes lacks a label, but experts reckon he belongs to the Schuco family.

SCHREYER & CO. (SCHUCO)

Miniature Bears

Great Little Bears

"Perhaps Schuco's greatest claim to fame," Barnaby went on, "is its miniature bears." "Like me?" asked Junior. "No, much smaller. They began in 1924 with the Piccolo range, tiny jointed bears only 2¾ in (6 cm) tall but with all the character of their big brothers. They were made with internal metal frames, and mohair specially clipped to keep their fur in scale with their little bodies. These delightful mini-bears had a maxi-success, and soon included tiny versions of the Yes/No bear and handbag companions with concealed scent bottles or powder compacts. By the 1930s they were a little larger, up to 3½ in (7.5 cm)." "Real little charmers, like me," concluded Junior.

LEFT AND BELOW: These are pocket-sized pals to accompany you anywhere. The 1930s bear on the left comes complete with boots just made for walking, but his three pals below, from the early 1930s, are happy to stay put! Note the range of colours: Schuco miniatures came in gold, red, green or lilac.

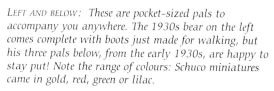

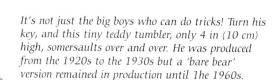

It's not just the big boys who can do tricks! Turn his key, and this tiny teddy tumbler, only 4 in (10 cm) high, somersaults over and over. He was produced from the 1920s to the 1930s but a 'bare bear' version remained in production until the 1960s.

SCHREYER & CO. (SCHUCO)

RIGHT AND LEFT: A Schuco miniature could have hidden assets, as two 1930s models demonstrate. Unscrew the head of the lilac-coloured bear, and his body opens out to form a powder compact and lipstick. And when the little gold chap loses his head, it reveals a hollow body containing a perfume bottle. Schuco also made a bear to contain jam or marmalade. No doubt Paddington would approve!

LEFT: Pre-1930s miniatures have tiny felt paws and feet. Later models' limbs end in stumps. Paws may be tricky on this scale, but the tiny faces still have room for little black beady eyes, stitched noses and mouths – and a cheeky expression.

BELOW: A 1930s family group ranging from 5 1/2 in (14 cm) to 7 in (18 cm), displays a new design with long nose and wide-set ears.

RIGHT: Squeeze this little fellow, and you'll get a fragrant surprise! Perfume sprays from his mouth, from the atomizer concealed by his plump body. A metal cap underneath allows his supply to be topped up.

GEBRÜDER BING

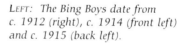

From Kitchenware To Bears

"Right, Junior," cried Barnaby, "when does a saucepan lead to a teddy bear?" "I can't imagine!" replied the puzzled youngster. "The answer," explained Barnaby, rather pleased with his riddle, "is when it's made by Gebrüder Bing! This German firm started out in 1865 making metal kitchenware. Over the years this led them to tin toys, from toy stoves and sewing machines to marvellous clockwork trains and boats. Naturally they followed the fashion and added soft toys to their range, and in the early 1900s their first teddy bears appeared on the market. Early Bing bears were modelled on the Steiff pattern, but eventually, in 1909 (by which time the one-time saucepan-smiths had become the world's biggest toy manufacturer), Steiff took legal action to stop them copying the famous button-in-ear trademark. Soon Bing turned their mastery of mechanical toys to their teddies. They made clockwork bears which walk, climb, skate, play ball or do somersaults." "Gosh," interrupted Junior. "So Bing goes boing! Didn't Steiff have a somersaulting bear?" "They did," Barnaby agreed, and that led to another court case between the two firms. Bing also specialized in costumed bears in colourful outfits. In 1932 the firm went bankrupt; their bears are now highly collectable." "A Bing's the thing," concluded Junior.

LEFT: The Bing Boys date from c. 1912 (right), c. 1914 (front left) and c. 1915 (back left).

RIGHT: The amazing acrobat, one of Bing's famous clockwork bears. Made c. 1910, he's still fit enough to perform his gymnastic tricks when his left arm is wound up.

LEFT TO RIGHT: Bing labels in order of age, starting with the ear button which Bing was banned from using in 1909. Next came an arrow-shaped tag, followed by an under-arm button (like the orange and white one shown here, or with the trademark 'GBN'). The last label in our series is the one used from 1919.

GEBRÜDER BING

Bing Bear, 1912

Without the identifying button, it is easy to mistake a Bing for a Steiff – but a true early Bing may be the rarer, and even more valuable, specimen. This 1912 Bing bear has his precious trademark button firmly fixed in place under his arm; though technically we should describe it as a stud, Steiff having claimed sole right to the term 'button'.

EARS Small, neat, rounded and wide-spaced, contributing their part to the dainty features characteristic of this family.

EYES Greyish-blue glass, secured with wire shanks and set just outside the face seams.

MUZZLE Long, like his Steiff contemporaries, but rather blunter and flatter-topped than Steiff style. The mohair of the muzzle is clipped short.

HUMP Very much reduced, producing a doll-like, nearly straight back, although the earliest Bings had a pronounced hump, copied from the Steiff bears. The body is quite long and narrow.

BELOW: Tired of being studied, our subject is off for a walk with a younger, if taller cousin. His companion, from the 1920s, shows a development in Bing style, with bigger ears, longer muzzle, and a wider smile, formed by longer mouth stitches.

ARMS AND LEGS Both are long (especially the arms) and slightly tapered. Long paws and large feet have beige felt pads, with claws stitched in rust thread to match the nose.

NOSE Bing noses tend to be distinctive, and this is a characteristic design. The vertically stitched nose, in rust thread, has its edges neatened with a double row of edging, and five central stitches extend down to the simple inverted V mouth.

GEBRÜDER BING

Bingo Sees It Through

Who could resist Bingo's gentle appeal and sweet expression?
Well, his first owner could. Bingo's dreams of a loving
home fell by the wayside back in the 1920s. The handsome young
bear just couldn't compete with the rather scruffy but adored
teddy-in-residence. But 70 years later, a quiet life brought its
rewards. He had kept his fur in fine fettle, his felt pads hardly
worn and complete with all claws, and even his growl intact,
and these days finds himself very much sought-after as a
precious pensioner.

*LEFT: Only a few years separate
these two Bings, but what a contrast
in style! The white teddy, from
c. 1915, has the daintier
features of earlier models,
contrasting with the long
nose and big ears of her
brown companion,
from c. 1918.*

GEBRÜDER BING

"I spy with my little eye,"
chanted Junior happily,
"something beginning with B."
"Bear? Bing? Barnaby? Button?"
hazarded his uncle.
"No – a Bruin Brigade,"
chuckled the youngster.

LEFT: A friendly wave from an early
1920s bear. Note his lovely dense
fur. Bing favoured the use of this
longer mohair during the 1920s.

LEFT: These adorable twins lived
with the same family from 1919
until their recent acquisition by a
lucky collector.

RIGHT: Big Bill, a handsome 24 in
(61 cm) giant from the 1920s,
shows off the unusual but
effective style of nose stitching
favoured by Bing.

GERMAN FAMILY TREE

Pawprints On The Sands Of Time

"Some of the most important pages in our family album," Barnaby reminded Junior, "are those devoted to the German branch. These are bears who left their pawprints on history. Who knows, if it had not been for German manufacturers, the American craze for bears might have gone the way of Billy Possum and other unsung non-heroes."

"With some ninety years of German history set out before us," Barnaby continued, "it is fascinating to see how little the basic design has changed. Look at old ever-so-many-greats-uncle Wolfgang. As early as 1904, he's distinctly a teddy bear, rather than the ancestral, more naturalistic bear toy. Not until the second half of this century can we detect any dramatic change of image, when our very youngest cousins developed a more self-conscious approach to creating a cuddly appearance.

1904

Wolfgang tugged at everyone's heartstrings when he took up his bow.

1920s

Fritz put on his best shirt and a new tie for his trip to the photographer.

1920s

Helmut, in his vest and string tie, was something of a tough guy.

1940s

Dear old Uncle Ludwig with his faithful hot-water bottle and smaller companion.

1950s

Teddy boy Hans was head over heels in love with a certain young lady…

1950s

…and here she is, lovely Frieda, in the bonnet he bought her one memorable spring day.

1960s

Johann's easy smile bears a message of peace and love from the Swinging Sixties.

c. 1907

Kurt was too late to be one of Roosevelt's Rough-Riders, but a bear could dream!

1910

With his nose in the air, Erich rather looked down on bears who were not Bing.

1920s

Dieter looks wistful as he relives his early happy cubhood days.

1937

Cheerful but with his tongue firmly in his cheek Gunther was the life and soul of every party.

1930s

Cousin Reinhard was a hero of the race-tracks – but a bit of roadhog on the public highway.

1940s

Otto, a chilly mortal, would not take off his woolly hat and scarf for his photo.

1940s

Gretel was a good conversationalist who could talk on all kinds of subjects.

1970s

Haughty Konrad went to a good school, and still wears his old school tie.

1980s

Little Franz is still rather small, 'bearly' old enough to have met all his relations.

1990

Thoroughly modern Bertold lists his hobbies as fashion, frisbies and fishing.

1992

A bouncing baby bear, Kiri is already keen to meet as many of her relatives as possible.

FLYING BEARS

Those Daring Young Bears In Their Flying Machines

"What are you looking at?" Barnaby asked. "That plane up there!" cried Junior. "I wish I could fly!" "Perhaps you may," reflected Barnaby; "there are several pilots in the family." "I'd fly through the air with the greatest of ease!" cried Junior, a daring young bear.

BELOW: Hurrah for the open sky again! Sopwith sets off on his first flight for 75 years.

· Sopwith ·

Second Lieutenant Arthur Turnbull, of the Royal Flying Corps, died in 1917, leaving his faithful bear Sopwith grounded. Three-quarters of a century later, Sopwith flew again in a Tornado, thanks to the British Royal Air Force's Treble One Squadron, also celebrating a 75th anniversary.

FLYING BEARS

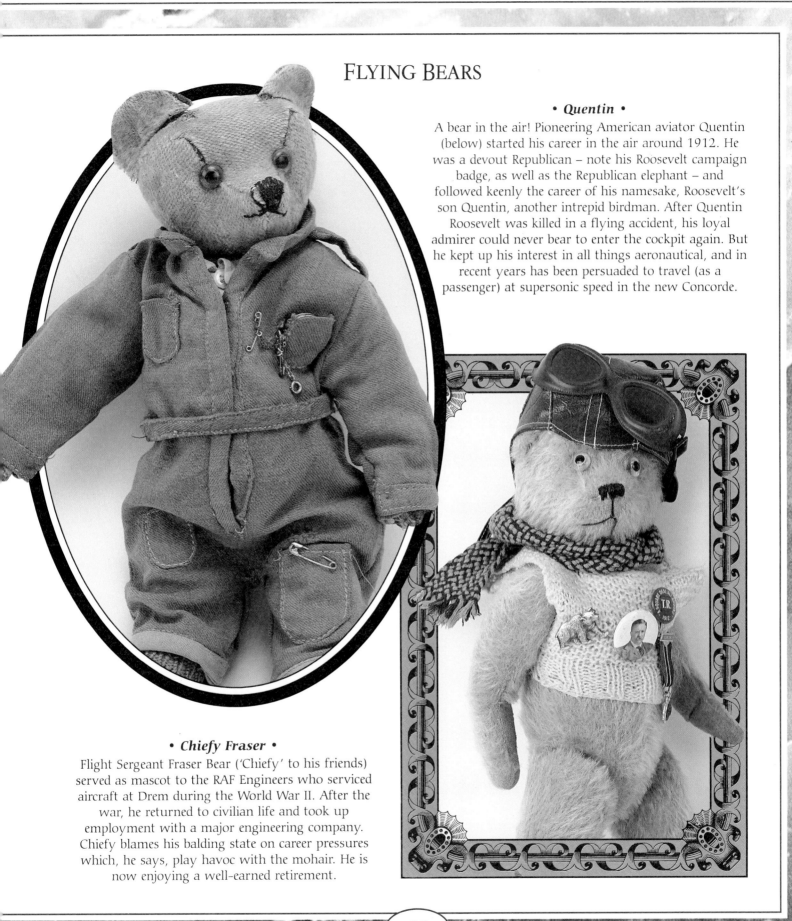

• Quentin •

A bear in the air! Pioneering American aviator Quentin (below) started his career in the air around 1912. He was a devout Republican – note his Roosevelt campaign badge, as well as the Republican elephant – and followed keenly the career of his namesake, Roosevelt's son Quentin, another intrepid birdman. After Quentin Roosevelt was killed in a flying accident, his loyal admirer could never bear to enter the cockpit again. But he kept up his interest in all things aeronautical, and in recent years has been persuaded to travel (as a passenger) at supersonic speed in the new Concorde.

• Chiefy Fraser •

Flight Sergeant Fraser Bear ('Chiefy' to his friends) served as mascot to the RAF Engineers who serviced aircraft at Drem during the World War II. After the war, he returned to civilian life and took up employment with a major engineering company. Chiefy blames his balding state on career pressures which, he says, play havoc with the mohair. He is now enjoying a well-earned retirement.

ADVENTURE BEARS

Dangerous Living!

"Bears don't need to go to war, or to sea, to lead adventurous lives," Barnaby remarked. "Our pioneering spirit has always found us eager to accompany our loved ones anywhere, and we can bear hardship better than most." Junior bounced excitedly at his opening remarks, but looked dubious at the mention of hardships. "I don't mind small adventures," he said, "but a big one might be a bit much to bear. I wouldn't like to end up with the mohair surgeons!"

Left: Donald Campbell's daughter Gina shared the passion of her father and her grandfather Malcolm, the fastest man on land. Here, Mr Whoppit encourages 'the last Campbell' in her own 1985 attempt on the World Water Speed Record.

• *Mr Whoppit* •

Mr Whoppit, on the left was a popular 1950s bear based on a cartoon character. He lived the fast life as companion of Donald Campbell, world land and water speed record-holder. Faithful unto death, he was with Campbell on his last record attempt when their boat Bluebird crashed. Saved by his lightweight kapok stuffing, Whoppit floated to the surface; his master's body was never found. Since then, Campbell's speed records have been broken, but Mr Whoppit retains his title of the world's fastest bear.

ADVENTURE BEARS

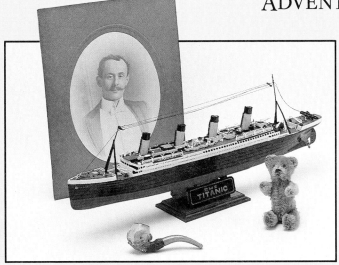

ABOVE: In 1912, Gatti, a little 6 in (15 cm) Bing bear, sailed on the Titanic, but somehow survived the wreck in which his master Gaspare Luigi Gatti, and more than 1,500 others, died. The 80th anniversary of the disaster was commemorated by Merrythought with a limited edition replica of the Titanic Bear.

• Stanley •

Like his namesake the great explorer, Stanley travelled far and wide. But after a Grand Tour of Europe and no fewer than seven excursions to Egypt, his health began to give way and he retired to England for repairs. These days, he's content to sit and tell travellers' tales.

• Fluffy •

Fluffy never even left London, but his adventure was perhaps the most remarkable of all. 'Homing' cats and dogs sometimes hit the news when they manage to locate their owners hundreds of miles away. It's harder for a teddy bear, but Fluffy found his way home across the city against the odds! His first owners, in North London, outgrew him and sent him to a jumble sale. Rehoused in central London, he was safe for a while, but in time found himself back on the jumble sale circuit. Somehow, he manoeuvred himself into a sale on the other side of the city. How did he know his original owner, now grown up, would be there? Recognizing his lopsided features and misleadingly sad expression, she bought him back. He has remained with her ever since, and though his look remains mournful, his travels have brought him happiness at last.

ENGLISH TEDDY BEARS

How The Bears Came Back To Britain

"Let's build a sand bear!" said Junior. "Good idea," replied Barnaby. "But I hope no-one will knock him down." "Then," retorted the irrepressible Junior, "he would be the first wild bear in Britain for about one thousand years!" Realizing the impossibility of squashing the cheeky cub, Barnaby, a teddy rather fond of the sound of his own growl, decided to embark on a lecture instead. "As you say," he began, "the last wild bears in Britain are believed to have lived in Scotland until about the year AD 1000. After that there were no native bears until the first British teddies appeared in 1908 or thereabouts. German teddies, most of them made by Steiff, were, however, imported before then. They had coats made from mohair plush woven in English mills which was therefore sometimes called 'Yorkshire cloth', or simply 'teddy bear cloth'. Perhaps inspired by the fact that Britain then had a very popular king, 'Teddy', King Edward VII, British toymakers soon decided to make their own bears. The first jointed, mohair plush bear made in Britain is generally believed to have been created by the London maker J.K. Farnell & Company in 1908. Unfortunately, most early British makers did not label their bears, so as well as being rare, they are difficult to identify," Junior sighed. "Now can we build that sandbear?" he asked.

TOP RIGHT: The small, boxed bear dates from c. 1917.

LEFT AND ABOVE RIGHT: Popular postcards showed teddies in many different roles, such as the golfer and standard bearer.

RIGHT: Miss Nightingale, the earliest identifiable British teddy, dates from 1912. The drummer is a Merrythought bear, one of the best known British firms.

ENGLISH TEDDY BEARS

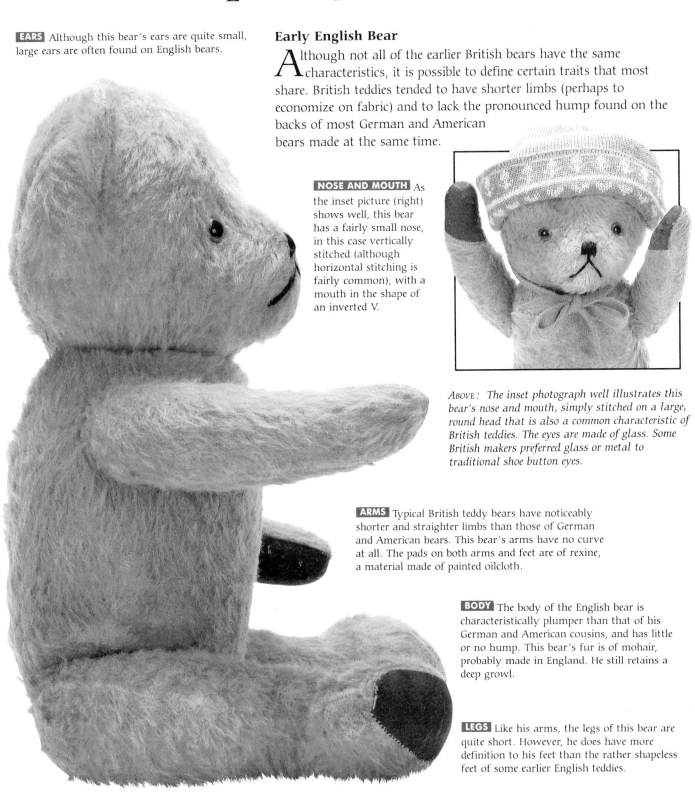

EARS Although this bear's ears are quite small, large ears are often found on English bears.

Early English Bear

Although not all of the earlier British bears have the same characteristics, it is possible to define certain traits that most share. British teddies tended to have shorter limbs (perhaps to economize on fabric) and to lack the pronounced hump found on the backs of most German and American bears made at the same time.

NOSE AND MOUTH As the inset picture (right) shows well, this bear has a fairly small nose, in this case vertically stitched (although horizontal stitching is fairly common), with a mouth in the shape of an inverted V.

ABOVE: The inset photograph well illustrates this bear's nose and mouth, simply stitched on a large, round head that is also a common characteristic of British teddies. The eyes are made of glass. Some British makers preferred glass or metal to traditional shoe button eyes.

ARMS Typical British teddy bears have noticeably shorter and straighter limbs than those of German and American bears. This bear's arms have no curve at all. The pads on both arms and feet are of rexine, a material made of painted oilcloth.

BODY The body of the English bear is characteristically plumper than that of his German and American cousins, and has little or no hump. This bear's fur is of mohair, probably made in England. He still retains a deep growl.

LEGS Like his arms, the legs of this bear are quite short. However, he does have more definition to his feet than the rather shapeless feet of some earlier English teddies.

ENGLISH TEDDY BEARS

Bears In Fashion: Bears In Wartime

By 1909 teddy bears had become so popular in Britain that many London stores featured them in elaborate window displays. They became fashion accessories, carried by well-dressed ladies or even worn in the form of jewellery. They appeared on postcards and in books, and were seen as motor car mascots. During World War I, of course, the importation of teddies from Germany ceased; thus, one of the few happy results of that tragic conflict was a considerable boost for the British soft toy industry. Small companies sprang up, flourished for a time, and then joined forces, resulting in the emergence of several of the major British makers, including Chad Valley, Merrythought and Pedigree, in the immediate post-war years.

LEFT: *This 'austerity' bear was produced in Britain around the period of World War II. As an economy measure, ordinary fabric was used instead of traditional fur fabric on the body. The bear was intended to be dressed.*

BELOW: *This mighty 'hug' of bears represents the collection of Peter and Francis Fagan of Colour Box Miniatures Ltd, who live on the Scottish borders. They produce miniature clay models of their bears.*

ENGLISH TEDDY BEARS

Mohair plush, the standard material for teddy bears, was of mainly British manufacture, and in the 1920s British makers further encouraged home (or, in this case, British Empire) industries by introducing kapok, a soft fibre derived from the seed pod of a tropical tree, as a filling for teddies. British makers used kapok instead of the harder, heavier wood wool, made from thin wood shavings, for body filling, but sometimes retained excelsior, which permitted better modelling, as a head filling.

Teddy Bear Aristocracy

These British bears were purchased by a collector on either side of the Atlantic. Anastasia (left) came from a teddy bear convention in Baltimore, Maryland. The Duke of Portobello was bought in the Portobello Road, London. However, similarities in style, identical head construction and cardboard sole inserts in the feet, show that they are brother and sister.

ABOVE CENTRE: Hand-made Cricket Ted is the mascot of the famouse Essex County Cricket Club.

LEFT: Brother Ted, a two-tone clown bear of 1925, is able to stand because of his firm stuffing of wood wool.

ABOVE: This group of small teddies dates from the World War II period. The bear second from left has a cloth body. The largest is a home-made bear probably based on one of the many do-it-yourself patterns published during the war years. He may not be beautiful but what an appealing expression he has.

MERRYTHOUGHT

Bears Of The Highest Quality

"Merrythought," declared Barnaby, "is one of the most famous British bear makers." "Am I a Merrythought bear?" asked Junior hopefully. "Merry," said Barnaby, "but I don't detect much thought." He went on. "It had its origins in a mohair mill set up in 1919 in Coalbrookdale (now Ironbridge), Shropshire. In the later 1920s its founders, W.G. Holmes and G.H. Laxton, found sales dropping in the face of new synthetic fibres. Soft toys offered a new way to use their mohair, and in 1930 they set up the Merrythought company. A.C. Janisch of J.K. Farnell and C.J. Rendel of Chad Valley joined the new company but it was deaf-mute designer Florence Atwood who was responsible for the first range of soft toys that appeared in 1931, including designs in golden mohair: the Magnet range in four sizes and the more expensive Merrythought line.

Merrythought's bears from the 1930s are now eagerly sought after by collectors. Like other toymakers, the company turned largely to war production in 1939–1945. At first the company's soft toys were made almost entirely by hand, and not until 1955 was an automatic stuffing machine introduced. As well as bears Merrythought has made character animals, felt dolls, rocking horses and push-along toys. Its bears are noted for their very high quality.

BELOW FAR LEFT: Merrythought's Bingie Boy and Bingie Girl of c. 1934 have bodies of velveteen with heads and lower arms of mohair. With them is a Bingie Cub, first introduced in 1931, whose unjointed legs keep him in a sitting position.

BELOW CENTRE: Punkinhead, with his striking topknot, was a bear made specially for Eaton's Department Store, Toronto, Canada, in 1949-1956.

LEFT: Peter Bear, with unjointed legs, was only briefly in production in 1962-1963 and is now rare.

MERRYTHOUGHT

Merrythought Bear, 1930s

Chummy was one of the first bears produced after the foundation of the Merrythought company in 1930. He has a button showing the maker's trademark (see far left) in his left ear. Merrythought later had to change the position of the button, to avoid copying Steiff's well-established "button-in-ear" trademark. Except for his nose, where wood wool is used, he is stuffed with kapok.

MUZZLE Short, pointed and close-clipped, Chummy's muzzle is quite worn. Some other Merrythought bears have a longer stitch extending upward at each end of the nose.

EYES Wide apart and set low down on the face, the eyes make the forehead appear high and broad. They are made of amber glass, with black pupils painted on the back surface.

EARS Large, rather flat ears, set fairly far back on his well-rounded head, give Chummy a typically English appearance.

ABOVE: Merrythought is an archaic English word for a wishbone, symbolizing a wish come true. A celluloid-covered metal button bearing the trademark was originally sewn in the ear, then moved to the back, before being abandoned.

BODY Short, rounded bodies are typical of English bears and give them an added 'cuddly' quality. Notice that Chummy has no hump on his back.

ARMS Fairly long and quite plump, curving gently towards the paws, which have felt pads. Four claws are blanket stitched on each of the pads.

LEGS Quite short, but well defined, with fairly thick thighs and well modelled ankles. A Merrythought label (bottom right) is stitched to the felt pad on the right foot.

ABOVE: Colin (right), shown here with his friend Chummy and a carrousel, was one of the Magnet range of the early 1930s. His arms are short and his ears small and round.

LEFT: This Merrythought bear in pastel blue mohair dates from the 1930s, when coloured bears, very often in blue or pink, were extremely popular.

RIGHT: The original button tag was replaced by labels sewn to the foot such as the rectangular woven label from the 1930s (bottom), and the post-World War II label (top).

MERRYTHOUGHT
IRONBRIDGE. SHROPS.
MADE IN ENGLAND

MERRYTHOUGHT
HYGIENIC TOYS
MADE IN ENGLAND

MERRYTHOUGHT

ABOVE LEFT AND RIGHT: Merrythought's Edwardian Bear was made in 1984 for the American market. Notice how closely the design of the head – wide, with long muzzle – resembles that of the bear of 1935 with the smart hat.

RIGHT: Merrythought bears of the 1960s: a brown bear in synthetic plush; his companion in gold mohair plush. The label seen on the foot of the latter reads 'Merrythought, Ironbridge, Shrops, Made in England'.

LEFT: As well as collectable bears, Merrythought has continued to make traditional teddies like this fine specimen. His large head and ears, and short limbs, are much like those of his 1930s ancestors.

Merrythought's Modern Bears

From the later 1950s onward, Merrythought persevered with its Bingie and 'M' series bears while also introducing a range of Walt Disney characters. Its Diamond Jubilee bear of 1990 aroused great interest among toy collectors, and today many Merrythought bears are made for the collectors' market: all hand-made and often in limited editions.

MERRYTHOUGHT

BELOW: A most colourful line-up, Merrythought produced these miniature, fully-jointed bears (from left) in red, brown-tipped, cream, brown and pink mohair, in a limited edition in 1992.

BELOW: Who could resist the charm of Merrythought's Mischief Bear? His designer was inspired by the contrition of a youngster who had broken a window.

BELOW: Master Mischief's rear view reveals the reason for his disgrace and his appeal for forgiveness. He has created mayhem with the catapult that dangles from his paws. A Miss Mischief also appeared in 1992.

Cheeky Bears

Cheeky: A Bear With Attitude

Merrythought's Cheeky is aptly named, with his wide, impish grin and tinkling metal bells sewn inside both ears. Cheeky appeared in 1957. The concept of this character bear perhaps stemmed from the Punkinhead (see page 90) made for a Canadian department store. Early Cheekies had fur of gold mohair or artificial silk plush. After 1960 they appeared in acrylic plush, and in various pastel colours as well as chocolate brown. Cheeky has been made as a nightdress case, as an open-mouthed bear (from 1962), and in 1966-1968 as a 'Twisty', featuring removable clothes on a body of fabric over a bendable interior frame.

ABOVE: A bear to warm the hands and the heart, the Cheeky muff first appeared in the 1950s. Note the large, broad, and fairly low-set ears, characteristic of Merrythought's Cheeky bears.

RIGHT: Cheeky gets into mischief.

MERRYT

LEFT: *Mr Twisty Cheeky appeared in 1966–1968. Built over a bendy frame, he could pose in various positions. Mr Twisty has a suede body and his trousers and braces are removable. Mrs Twisty wore a removable dress and pinafore.*

LEFT: *This 1992 version of Cheeky has fur of tipped, pastel-shaded mohair.*

BOTTOM: *This 1970s Cheeky has pads in a contrasting colour. Such velveteen pads are often found on Cheekies.*

FACING PAGE, BOTTOM RIGHT: *An early Cheeky prototype, this is the New Print Teddy of 1955. Her fabric body gives her the appearance of a dressed bear.*

LEFT: *A colour-contrasted pair of Cheekies dating from the 1950s strike a balance between a traditional colour and a more startling pastel shade!*

CHAD VALLEY

Toymakers To The Queen

"Now we come to some bears with a royal stamp," Barnaby announced. "The firm of Chad Valley began with stationery and went on to bear more interesting fruit." "Who was Mr Chad Valley?" asked Junior. "Not who, but where. In 1897 the firm moved to a Midlands factory called the Chad Valley Works, after the nearby Chad stream, and later adopted this trade name. It was here, in 1915-1916, that they expanded their range of products from board games to soft toys – including their first bear. They were soon established making traditional British-style bears. By the early 1930s they were offering 14 sizes of bear, some with a choice of hard or soft stuffing. By the end of the decade they were one of the world's leading toy manufacturers, and in 1938 earned the Royal Warrant of Appointment as 'Toymakers to Her Majesty the Queen'. (After 1953 the Royal Warrant referred to 'HM Queen Elizabeth, The Queen Mother') Like other firms, Chad Valley has moved with the times to adopt new materials and techniques and with such success that in 1960 they celebrated their centenary, and still prosper, though under new ownership."

BELOW: This Chad Valley Rainbow Tubby Bear, a novelty bear first made in 1926, came in several shades and once sported a clown collar, cap and bell.

Teddy Randell

Teddy Randell is a true Chad Valley bear, with his very British conformation and round head with the wide, rectangular nose so characteristic of this manufacturer. He began life in the role for which all teddies were designed, as a child's much loved companion – as his worn mohair and pads demonstrate. When little Sally-Ann, his owner, had to go into hospital, naturally Teddy Randell went too. One sad day a nurse picked him up and carried him off to a quiet room full of toys. Before he could begin to worry that he had reached the end of his useful career, an auction was in full swing and he found himself with a new owner – and a new career, for Teddy Randell had been bought to help raise money for the children's hospital in Edinburgh, Scotland, and has since dedicated his life to helping sick children everywhere.

CHAD VALLEY

Chad Valley Bear, 1950s

This appealing bear is one of the most recognizable designs produced by Chad Valley. Note what has become known as the Chad Valley nose: a tightly-bound, wide rectangle.

EYES Amber glass, wide set and stitched in position on the seams of the centre panel.

EARS Large, round and flat, and set well to the sides of the head, sewn into the seams.

HEAD Round, with a broad forehead. The profile appears almost flat. The muzzle is quite pronounced but almost hidden by dense, fluffy mohair.

NOSE AND MOUTH The nose is a characteristic tightly bound oblong of vertical stitches, the mouth sewn in the traditional inverted V.

ABOVE: Early Chad Valley bears were tagged with a button, usually in the right ear but sometimes on the chest or back. Several types are known. The commonest is this celluloid-covered metal stud, with the words 'Chad Valley British Hygienic Toys' printed in black.

ARMS AND LEGS Both are short. The arms are slightly curved, the legs solid and chunky and ending in short stubby feet.

BELOW AND BELOW RIGHT: An Aerolite button, 1923-1926, and a post-1953 label.

PADS Slightly worn rexine (artificial leather substitute, common in British bears) and of an unusual teardrop shape. Claws are absent.

BODY Typically British, short and round with a straight and humpless back.

CHAD VALLEY

LEFT: An early bear catches a plane! Big-eared Biggles dates from the 1920s. His large ears and long muzzle are typical Chad Valley style. More unusual is his nose, sewn in beige thread with horizontal stitches. On the right is a more traditional, vertically stitched nose set on a real rarity. Chad Valley made only six wine-coloured teddies in the 1930s. He still has the identifying button in his ear and the label on his foot.

BELOW RIGHT: One of the earliest surviving Chad Valley bears, from 1923.

BELOW LEFT: A box of delights, these bears have birthdates spanning three decades, from the 1930s to 1950s, but share an unmistakable family resemblance: round, flattish heads, long, blunt muzzles and large, wide-set ears.

CHAD VALLEY

RIGHT AND FAR RIGHT: Who needs mohair? During World War II, a mohair shortage produced the little fellow of sheepskin. By the 1960s, synthetic materials were gaining in popularity, producing equally cuddly bears like his friend, whose fur is acrylic.

BELOW RIGHT: A rare pair of 1930s bears flaunt flashily coloured fur, one yellow, one blue. But they're not sailing under false colours, for both these bears have their Chad Valley labels stitched to their feet!

ABOVE: Alex has something to smile about, having preserved his long, curly mohair plush in excellent condition since c. 1935. The brushed-cotton pads of his large feet have lasted well, too, as have his stitched claws (five on each foot and four per paw).

BELOW LEFT: Swinging a jaunty paw is a mohair ted from the Swinging Sixties, though he doesn't seem to have shopped in Carnaby Street!

FAR LEFT: Oh my poor feet! Enjoying a well-earned rest is footsore Felix, whose worn-out pads look as if he just kept on walking since he left the factory in 1930. Years of service have also worn away most of the bristles on his close-shaven muzzle.

Cubby Bear

Cubby Cuts A Dash

Introduced in the mid-1930s, the Cubby Bear stays fixed in a sitting position by his unjointed legs. He has large, painted glass eyes, a vertically stitched nose, felt pads and jointed arms which curve gently downwards. At first Cubbies came in shaggy alpaca plush or artificial-silk plush, but in the 1950s the rise of new materials led to nylon plush Cubbies in a range of colours.

ABOVE: Because Steiff claimed the button-in-ear trademark, later Chad Valley bears have the button stitched on the upper back.

RIGHT: A 1930s bear, in lovely condition for his age, preserves the enduring appeal of the Cubby range.

BELOW: Magna Maggie on the right dates from 1955. She has lost her identifying label but is clearly a member of the Magna clan – unlike her partner, who belongs to an older branch of the Chad Valleys, from the late 1920s.

Magna Bears

New Fashion In Noses

In the late 1930s and 1940s, Chad Valley produced another successful range in the Magna bears. Of similar body shape to their other Chad Valley relations, Magna bears feature a distinctive nose design: most of their family have the Chad Valley vertically stitched nose, but a Magna nose is composed of several horizontal stitches. This range is also distinguished by a blue and white woven 'Magna Series' label.

ABOVE: The label reads 'Chad Valley Magna Series, Harborne, England'. Harborne, in Birmingham, housed the main factory.

PEACOCK & Co.

A Short-lived Pride Of Peacocks

In 1931 Chad Valley bought up Peacock & Company Limited a long-established, small London firm manufacturing wooden toys, and for a few years produced a new range of bears under the Peacock label at the main Chad Valley factory.

ABOVE: Chad Valley's embroidered Peacock label features the open-tailed peacock of the original Peacock & Company logo.

RIGHT: A 1926 Peacock bear.

LEFT: A rare, early Peacock bear.

BELOW RIGHT: Another Peacock bear displays the typical vertically stitched nose, inverted V mouth and glass eyes.

J K FARNELL

Winnie The Pooh And Alpha Too

"In 1840 John Kirby Farnell founded a London business making household goods." "What does that have to do with bears?" interrupted Junior. "Don't be impatient," said Barnaby. "His daughter Agnes, aided by her brother Henry, switched the firm's interest to soft toys, and by 1908 the firm achieved a place in teddy history by producing what are believed to be the first English teddy bears. These quickly became one of the firm's best-selling products, marketed from the early 1920s as Alpha bears (named after the Alpha works built in 1921). They are distinguished bears of high-quality manufacture. Humped backs, long muzzles and the distinctive closing central seam down the stomach recall their Steiff cousins in Germany. In 1921 a Farnell bear was purchased by Dorothy Milne for her son Christopher Robin's first birthday, and became Winnie the Pooh, world-renowned hero of A.A. Milne's best-selling books.

ABOVE: Not just a pretty face, one of the Farnell tribe settles down at the typewriter to record his version of the family history. Made in the 1920s, this jaunty little fellow looks as though he still has plenty of get up and go. The amount of wear and tear on his mohair fur tells us that this is one teddy who surely fulfilled his role as a child's much loved companion!

BELOW: Farnell bears dating from the 1920s to the 1950s meet up for a reunion. Despite the range of mohair (curly, shaggy and short pile), a family resemblance is seen in hand-sewn noses and mouths, which retain a consistent style.

J K FARNELL

NOSE AND MOUTH Hand-sewn, giving each bear a unique expression. The broad nose with vertical stitches is typical of Farnell bears.

HEAD Large and round-faced, with broad brow and wide-set glass eyes. Unlike the flat muzzle of most British bears, his snout is long like a real bear's, though less pointed than that of the equally long-nosed Steiff models.

ARMS Long, tapering and almost straight, with an upward, 'hugging' curve at the wrist. Here again the modelling resembles that of Steiff bears.

PAWS Narrow wrists and long, curved paws. The felt pads boast hand-sewn joined claws in blanket-stitch, typical also of Merrythought and W.J. Terry bears.

EARS Smallish, wide-spaced and slightly cupped inwards.

BODY The naturalistic humped back is more characteristic of German than British design.

LEGS Long, with rounded thighs, thin ankles and large, narrow feet.

Farnell Bear, 1930s

Farnell bears rarely retain the trademark label, but are identifiable by the characteristic shape and high quality of fabric and manufacture. The silky gold mohair plush on this wistful, elderly gentleman retains its original sheen and texture. Farnell prided themselves on using only top-quality materials.

LEFT: The Alpha label, introduced in the early 1920s, had the words woven in blue silk on a white ground and was stitched to a foot-pad. Few early bears retain the tag.

J K FARNELL

Fired With Enthusiasm

"Come on, Junior," Barnaby encouraged. "We'll need to get a move on if we want to meet all your Farnell cousins." "You go that way and I'll go this." said Junior. "You know, collectors rate them as the best of British bears," Barnaby went on. "They fought back after the factory burned down in 1934…" ("The true 'grin and bear it' spirit," murmured Junior.) "…and were back in force by the next spring. Farnell bears continued to be made until 1968."

LEFT: *In the 1920s, media excitement at reports of the Abominable Snowman (Yeti) inspired Farnell's slightly sinister, earless 'Yeti' bear.*

"Well, you have to admire the Farnell family," Junior admitted. "That factory fire just doesn't bear thinking of!"

BELOW: *A 1926 Alpha bear in long, curly, cinnamon-tipped mohair plush is very like its Steiff rival of the same period.*

LEFT: *Three 1920s Farnell brothers in fine fettle for their age. Note the rare (and highly collectable) lavender hue of the bear on the right. His big brother, behind, is noteworthy for an unusual nose: a semi-circular outline, filled in with vertical satin stitch (instead of the typical oblong nose).*

J K FARNELL

RIGHT: Another Steiff-like 1920s Farnell bear enjoys sitting in comfort, thanks to her articulated joints, connected to each other with metal rods.

FAR RIGHT: The decline of German influence. This late 1920s Farnell bear shows a more English style with flatter muzzle and shorter limbs.

LEFT: No label, but it is a feather in the cap of this 1930s bear (left) to know he is a true Farnell.

RIGHT: Wear and tear have exposed this early Farnell's front seam, used, uniquely to Farnell and their German rival Steiff, in preference to the back seam for insertion of stuffing.

BELOW: Where's the fire? This 1927 Farnell bear is ready for action with his fire engine – hardly surprising when you consider he is just six years younger than that highly active bear, Winnie the Pooh himself. The original Pooh Bear now lives in retirement among his books in the New York Public Library.

JK FARNELL

LEFT: *Poor Threadbear, a 1930s Farnell, has had his fur loved right off but is otherwise quite well for his age.*

BELOW: *This happy couple both date back to the 1930s, but bow-tied Bernard features the earlier head shape with long nose, while his lady friend's muzzle is more fashionably short, in the British style. However, Bernard boasts the prestigious Alpha Toy label on his left foot, whereas the lady has to rely on her good looks to prove her right to the Farnell name.*

J K FARNELL

LEFT: *Little bears have always been popular. A 1930s example in cinnamon mohair diverges from the usual Farnell pattern with his aberrant head shape, low-slung ears and short limbs.*

BELOW: *This bear is a more typical 1940s small Farnell.*

LEFT: *Compton dates from the 1920s and needs no trademark to make him instantly recognizable as a Farnell.*

FAR LEFT AND LEFT: *A later label from the 1930s has a shield motif printed in red and blue. In its final years of production Farnell dropped the Alpha trade name. This last label also shows the move from London to Hastings, begun in 1959 and complete in 1964 – only four years before production ceased.*

CHILTERN (HG STONE & Co.)

Huggable Hordes From The Hills

"The next firm we have to consider," Barnaby announced, "might be said to be a cousin of Farnell. In 1919 Leon Rees inherited his father's toy works in Buckinghamshire, in the Chiltern Hills." "I suppose the Chilly Hills were full of polar bears," Junior interposed. "Certainly not," said Barnaby sternly. "Brown bears, once, but that was a thousand years before the Chiltern Toy Works. As I was saying, Farnell influence soon came to bear when Leon joined up with Farnell's Harry Stone. The company became H.G. Stone & Company, but kept its Chiltern trademark. One of its early successes, from about 1923, was the Hugmee teddy bear, which stayed popular until Chad Valley took over the firm in 1967. Hugmee bears pride themselves on being particularly cuddly, because of the soft kapok filling. You can always tell your Hugmee cousins by the posture. They all sit exactly the same way, heads hanging. They have an excuse, since their squashy stuffing can't support their big, heavy heads properly, but don't let me catch you copying them: chin up, and look as if you're paying attention." "Oh, I am, honestly," Junior protested. "I shall know Hugmee bears because they're huggable."

LEFT: Chiltern tricycle teddies of 1955 were often based on media star bears. We may not recognize the cyclist on the far left, but his companion, TV star Sooty, remains highly popular today.

LEFT: This silk-plush skater of 1935 comes complete with skates, sweater and muff.

RIGHT: Master Teddy, was in 1915 the Chiltern firm's first teddy. His wide smile and bulbous eyes give an endearingly dopey look.

CHILTERN (HG STONE & Co.)

Hugmee Bear, 1960s

Very similar to earlier Hugmees; his ancestors might appreciate minor developments in the form of a realistic, plastic nose (first used on Chiltern bears in 1958) and plastic, lock-in safety eyes.

HEAD Large, round, with a flat back and blunt, longish muzzle giving a characteristically triangular profile. The typical droop of the head is caused by the soft kapok stuffing failing to provide support at the neck and is almost a recognizable Chiltern trademark in its own right.

EARS Large, round, very wideset. Gathering at the base creates a naturalistic shape.

EYES Amber plastic, fixed to the face seam.

PADS Large, tear-shaped velveteen. Four separate claws are created with straight stitch on the forepaws, and five on the feet. The footpads are reinforced with card.

LEGS Good solid legs giving a stable base. Much shorter and fatter than the arms, with plump thighs and pronounced ankles, they add to the comfortingly sturdy effect.

BELOW: Chiltern bears did not acquire permanent cloth labels with the tradename until the 1940s. In 1915, their first bear, Master Teddy, bore an unassuming circular cardboard tag which hung on a string on his chest. It does not even feature the now famous Chiltern name.

ARMS Long, quite thick and tapering towards the wrist, with a pronounced upward curve.

ABOVE CENTRE: A cardboard tag was attached to the first Chiltern bears. The round orange tag features a drawing of the Chiltern hills where the bears continued to be made until 1940, when the factory was turned over to war work.

ABOVE: When Chad Valley took over the firm in 1967, they kept the well-known Chiltern name and marketed the bears as 'Chad Valley Chiltern Hygienic Toys'. The 'hygienic' claim had long been part of Chiltern marketing.

NOSE AND MOUTH The hand-sewn, shield-shaped nose of early Hugmees has given way to moulded plastic. The mouth is stitched with a small inverted V, creating an introspective expression which is highly typical of all Chiltern Hugmee bears.

CHILTERN (HG STONE & Co.)

TOP RIGHT: A 1976 Chad Valley/ Chiltern bear peers curiously down to watch his older Chiltern friends struggling with their maths homework.

LEFT: A 1955 unjointed teddy in gold mohair and his blond companion of unknown date work things out together. The latter has a mechanism in his tummy which makes a jingling sound when shaken.

Henry

In the face of all the evidence, Henry is a child of the 1960s, but he is all too obviously a bear born out of his time. Let others do as they please, Henry is going to hang on to his respectable one-piece costume (more Roaring Twenties than Swinging Sixties), his air of cautious reserve and his dour Chiltern expression. Here, we can see at once, is a bear who knows his own mind, and one who would not be seen dead shopping in Carnaby Street, sporting long hair or dancing at a disco to that shocking modern music. One feels any parent of the time who bought Henry could be confident that here at least old standards were preserved.

CHILTERN (HG STONE & Co.)

LEFT: Two Hugmee bears in gold mohair are outward bound on a bicycle not perhaps quite made for two. Big Brother is, of course, the older, from the 1940s, and features the original hand-stitched, shield-shaped nose. Little Brother, from the 1960s, has the newer plastic 'safety' nose held in place with a washer as safety regulations now recommended, though some of his contemporaries retained sewn noses.

RIGHT: "Hugmee," he said, so I did! Certainly the owners of these two bears managed to resist the temptation to hug their fur away. Big Bear dates from the 1940s; Little Bear is some ten years his junior.

LEFT: Not quite a song in his heart, but this 1940s bear has a musical box in his tummy to play a Brahms lullaby when his key is turned.

ABOVE: A little Chiltern bear from the 1930s cannot resist dancing when his younger cousin from the 1950s, one of several musical bears produced by Chiltern, strikes up a tune.

DEAN'S RAG BOOK Co.

From Rags To Riches

"Uncle Barnaby, Uncle Barnaby," cried Junior, "why are we visiting a rag book company? I thought we were studying family history!" "So we are, youngster," explained Barnaby with a superior smile. "Dean's Rag Book Company began indeed with rag books, back in 1903, but they were so successful they soon diversified. Bibs, kites, rag dolls..." "Rag bears?" demanded Junior. "Yes, that was how it began. In 1908 they came up with a 'Knockabout' printed teddy kit for people to make up at home, but in 1915 they produced their first catalogued bear: the mohair Kuddlemee. They went on to produce a wide range, including a Russian bear..." ("Rushin' where?" put in Junior),

"...a patriotic British bear called Tommy Fuzzbuzz, polar bears and black bears, and Bendy Bears with flexible 'evripose' joints." "Are they still inventing new kinds?" asked Junior. "I can't bear to think they might have run out of ideas." "On the contrary," Barnaby assured him, "in 1981 they started producing limited-edition collectors' bears which were a great success. They dropped the 'Rag Book' part of their name when they were taken over by Plaintalk in 1986, but, as The Dean's Company Limited, they still make teddies and are Britain's oldest toy manufacturer."

ABOVE: The famous Dean's trademark celebrates the durability of Dean's famous rag books, made 'for children who wear their food and eat their clothes' and shown withstanding a canine tug of war.

ABOVE AND RIGHT: An unusual little unjointed Dean's bear of the 1920s. A rather more sophisticated contemporary from the same firm still has his original label.

ABOVE: A barrowload of mischief! Three little Dean's bears from the 1940s and 1950s have cajoled a Chad Valley friend (in the hat) into joining their game. Note the variation in head shape: the standing bear has what became the characteristic Dean's head, round, with slightly defined muzzle.

DEAN'S RAG BOOK Co.

Dean's Bear, 1930s

When this delightful bear emerged from Dean's factory, teddy bears were only part of the company's production. Mickey Mouse, Felix the Cat, Peter Rabbit or Dismal Desmond were more in demand. With today's teddy renaissance, Dean's are noted for collectors' bears.

LEFT: Registered in 1910, Dean's bulldog-and-terrier trademark continued in use until 1965. However, a range of labels has been used.

BELOW LEFT: In the 1930s, Dean's teddies carried a printed cloth label sewn on the foot, with 'Made in England by Dean's Rag Book Co. Ltd, London' in brown lettering. Some early Dean's soft toys were identified by a metal button fixed to the body.

HEAD Quite large, round-faced, flat-topped and triangular in profile. A broad forehead slopes gently down into the longish, tapering muzzle.

EARS Moderately large and rather flat, and set well back on the very top of the bear's head.

EYES Translucent glass, large and rather bulbous, sewn in position on wire shanks.

BODY Straight-backed in true British style and, like many British bears, slightly floppy because of the soft wood wool and kapok stuffing.

ARMS Quite long for a British bear, with upward curving paws. The pads are velveteen, and somewhat worn. Three straight claws are stitched in double thread on the plush.

LEGS Also longish, with large feet, velveteen pads and stitched claws. The trademark label is stitched on to the left foot.

LEFT: From the 1960s, when the company moved to Rye, Sussex, Dean's Childsplay Toys (a Dean's Rag Book subsidiary firm) adopted the red heart logo.

DEAN'S RAG BOOK Co.

Razza

'Razza', an early Dean's bear with the Dean's logo stamped on his right foot, had a very confusing start in life. The shop which bought him thought he was a dog, the assistant who unpacked him thought he was a lion, but the little girl who bought him knew he was a bear. Razza hasn't stopped laughing since, his mouth open in a wide grin to show his little felt tongue. In fact, he's a comical fellow altogether, with his cartoon-style white muzzle, round, goggling eyes and quaint posture. A faithful companion throughout his mistress's childhood, he couldn't resist a joke on her wedding day, when he commandeered the chauffeur's seat and peaked cap in the wedding car.

BELOW: These realistic bears were created as part of Dean's 1950s Tru-to-Life series. The face is shaped over an internal rubber mask, and rubber is also used for the paws.

BELOW RIGHT: A group of post-1975 bears shows some variation. The two on the right have typical round, short-nosed faces whereas their friend has reverted to a long muzzle.

DEAN'S RAG BOOK

BELOW: Well may the famous 1930s Bertie preserve his wide, sweet, inverted T smile – for he is now known worldwide as one of the great classic bears of British toy manufacturing history.

RIGHT: A happy family! These four Dean's bears may date back to the mid to late 1930s, but they have lost none of their verve (and surprisingly little of their mohair coats) over the years.

ABOVE AND RIGHT: The bear goes from strength to strength! Young Michael represents the latest in Dean's bears, while the little keyboard virtuoso was created more than a generation earlier, in c. 1960.

Wendy Boston

The Boston Bath Party

"Now, Junior," announced Barnaby, "we come to a bear breakthrough: the invention of the first fully washable bear!" "Ugh," said Junior, who like many youngsters washes only under protest. Barnaby overrode him to explain, "The firm of Wendy Boston started up in Wales in 1946. From the start, safety was their watchword: in fact, soon they adopted the 'Playsafe' label. They invented screw-locked eyes instead of using easily broken wire shanks, and in 1954 produced the world's first machine-washable bear, nylon with foam stuffing. Mothers loved them because they were hygienic, and children because they were extra soft and cuddly. By the 1960s Wendy Boston claimed to make 28 per cent of all Britain's soft toy exports. But in 1976 growing competition forced their closure."

BELOW: Three 1950s unjointed Wendy Boston bears form a cuddlesome clan. The youngest, sitting on the right, is one of the new washable bears which revolutionized the soft toy industry.

WENDY BOSTON

Wendy Boston Bear, 1960s

From the 1950s, new Codes of Safety for toys emphasized hygiene, so all-synthetic Boston bears were a hit. This 1960s example does not look at all washed out, but he may have been through the washing-machine a good many times!

HEAD Characteristically large and round, with the famous safety eyes and a small, embroidered nose. The ears are cut as an integral part of the head – a bright design idea enabling them to be pegged to a washing-line without the risk of them coming off!

ARMS AND LEGS Simplicity is the keynote here. The limbs are short and sturdy, unjointed and fixed in an appealing outstretched pose. The stocky legs have no defined ankles or feet, with no claws delineated on the feet.

FUR Soft, washable, honey-coloured woven-nylon plush.

ABOVE: The printed label here gives washing instructions, other Wendy Boston labels specify a branded washing powder.

PAWS Simplicity again! These are made of the same fabric as the body, without definition. Three small claws are embroidered in black floss on each paw.

RIGHT: A 1960s jointed bear is not washable but has the traditional mohair body.

PEDIGREE SOFT TOYS Ltd

Bruins From Belfast

"Our next family," Barnaby announced, "can truly claim to take pride in its pedigree, for they were marketed as Pedigree Soft Toys. The Pedigrees were founded in the early 1930s as a subsidiary of Lines Brothers Limited, at that time the world's largest soft toy manufacturer. They were based in Merton, Surrey, but in 1946 the firm opened a factory in Belfast, Northern Ireland which became its soft toy base in 1955. So if you meet any Pedigree bear labelled 'Made in England' you will know he must have been made before 1955 – or after 1966, when the business transferred to Canterbury, Kent for its final years. Many of the post-1940 bears are real cosmopolitans, for Pedigree opened factories in New Zealand, South Africa and Australia as well." "How can I recognize a Pedigree bear?" Junior wanted to know. "Well, the early models are very distinctive. They have long heads with short muzzles, smiling faces with plastic noses, and short arms and legs. After 1960 they acquired a new look when they started being made with a longer muzzle created by a triangular insert. Pedigree continued in business under different owners until 1988."

LEFT: Cheeky Charmain, a 1950s Pedigree bear, sports an elegant hat but a rather less ladylike expression as she sticks out her little pink felt tongue.

BELOW RIGHT: Her brother Charles is more serious, as befits his more traditional design.

PEDIGREE SOFT TOYS Ltd

Irish Pixie

A leprechaun of a bear from the Belfast factory, early 1950s. With his upturned nose and pixie grin, he clearly won the heart of his owner, who hugged away most of his fur but lovingly replaced worn pads.

FUR Believe it or not, this was once a smart coat of mohair plush: traces remain on his sides and inner ear. He retains his smile, knowing that a worn bear is a loved bear. The erosion of the mohair gives us a good view of his construction, with doll-like straight back and limbs, bulbous head and that highly original snub nose.

ABOVE: A printed label from the 1950s, stitched into the top of the back seam, identifies a bear from the Belfast factory in Ireland.

ARMS AND LEGS Quite long and straight, with little shaping of the paws and round, stumpy feet. The pads are replacements, but the lack of claws original.

HEAD The classic round Pedigree head, with broad forehead, wide-spaced ears and glass eyes positioned well down the face.

NOSE Black plastic, above an inverted-T smiling mouth.

EARS Large, slightly cupped and sewn into the head seam. The poor chap's baldness makes them look larger than they really are!

PEDIGREE SOFT TOYS Ltd

BELOW: A 1950s Pedigree family picks up the pieces together, they don't seem to have got very far yet!

Walking, Talking, Living Bear

"I do like seeing all these relations, Uncle Barnaby," Junior exclaimed. "I'm only sorry we can't fit in more of them," Barnaby said. "We haven't seen Pedigree's battery-operated bears, like Simon the Walking Bear or the talking Rupert Bear. Such unusual relatives are in great demand, but rather elusive."

FAR RIGHT: Isn't it funny how a bear loves honey! Still in the 1950s, note Honey Bear's typical round head, minimalist muzzle and short limbs.

RIGHT: No date, but his pedigree is impeccable, as the long face, pleasant smile and short straight limbs clearly prove!

PEDIGREE SOFT TOYS Ltd

BELOW: Charlotte, on the left and Emmeline, on the right are two mohair misses from the 1950s who both feature the longer muzzle style adopted by later Pedigree bears.

LEFT: A more recent scion of the Pedigree family, this 1970s bear shows the new-style muzzle. He is rounder in both face and body than his forebears, but their short limbs and bluntish muzzle persist as a feature of this group.

BELOW: "Oh, my poor frayed paws! These family gatherings are quite exhausting. You won't mind if I don't stand up, will you?"

CANTERBURY BEARS

Canterbury Belles And Beaux!

"Great oaks from little acorns grow," quoted Barnaby, "and great companies may have small beginnings. In 1979, when commercial artist John Blackburn was asked to design a teddy bear for a young man's grandmother, he thought it was just another job – 'like designing a washing-machine,' he said! But he soon got hooked. In 1980 he and his wife set up Canterbury Bears, a family business which has won worldwide acclaim in a mere decade. To start with they flirted with other soft animals, but quickly realized it was at bears they excelled. Sticking to high-quality hand-crafted teddies, by 1985 they had earned not only a high reputation but the right to use the City of Canterbury official coat of arms, in recognition of their services both to local industry and to local charities." "Not a coat of paws?" asked Junior; but Barnaby ignored him. He went on firmly, "They are so proud of their bears they offer them free life insurance. Battered bears, no matter what the damage, can return for free repairs at any time. In 1991 they teamed up with Gund to distribute Canterbury bears in the United States, starting with ten new limited edition teddies."

BELOW RIGHT: Canterbury bears come in all styles and sizes, as demonstrated by this contrasting pair. The big brunette bruin in dark brown short pile mohair, and his cute little blond pal, Buttons, bear very little family resemblance! But both share high standards of manufacture, and both belong to the 1992 Canterbury International Range, marketed jointly by Gund and Canterbury, as the foot label makes clear.

ABOVE: Two more varieties from Canterbury's International Range, Brandy is a traditionalist in shape and colour, with plump body and honey-coloured fur. His trendy friend Rufus demonstrates not only a thoroughly modern shade of jazzy red mohair, but the fashionably long, slim body, smallish head and eyes, and long limbs in favour among artist bears of the 1990s.

CANTERBURY BEARS

Canterbury Bear, 1992

Traditionalism and modernism meet in the person of Ophelia. She has the long limbs, long muzzle, curved arms, well-defined feet and even the hump of her ancestors, yet her design is unmistakably modern, with a stylish pattern of round shapes repeated between head, ears and muzzle.

HEAD Rounded, with an almost surrealistically long muzzle, also rounded from the front view, but almost rectangular in profile.

EYES Replica shoe buttons, small and not a prominent feature of her face, much like those of real bears!

EARS Circular and enormous! Set on the sides of the head, they come more than halfway down her 'skull'.

BODY Fairly long and narrow. In profile the body forms an inverted triangle, with a prominent, squarish hump.

ARMS Very long and markedly curved. Unlike traditional design, Ophelia's arms curve from the 'elbow' rather than the 'wrist'. Her paws have long, curving pads made of suede.

LEGS Longish, narrow and very straight. She has well-defined, chunky feet with suede pads; note the label on the upturned pad.

ENGLISH FAMILY TREE

The Stately Bears Of England

"The English family is a cadet branch of the family tree," Barnaby reminded his nephew, "but nonetheless a very respectable branch." "O to bear in England now that April's here," murmured Junior. Barnaby looked at him. "The British bear," he continued sternly, "only became a true market force in World War I, when the import of German bears, their greatest rivals, was banned. By the time Germany was back in the market, British bears were well established."

1925

Sir Edward Grey was a trusted adviser to all the famous politicians of the day.

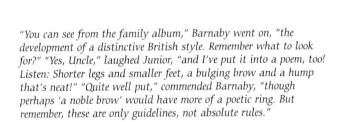

"You can see from the family album," Barnaby went on, "the development of a distinctive British style. Remember what to look for?" "Yes, Uncle," laughed Junior, "and I've put it into a poem, too! Listen: Shorter legs and smaller feet, a bulging brow and a hump that's neat!" "Quite well put," commended Barnaby, "though perhaps 'a noble brow' would have more of a poetic ring. But remember, these are only guidelines, not absolute rules."

1930s

Family ties were very important to Harold – he certainly had plenty of relatives.

1930s

Maurice was a farmer, but liked to add the odd touch of elegance to his appearance.

1960s

Cuddly Clive was a Beatles fan and grew his fur fashionably over his eyes.

1960s

His cousin Francis preferred the Monkees and was a real 'Daydream Believer'.

1970s

Simon has put on his thinking cap, but looks as though he finds it hard going.

1970s

Barry embarked on a career in the law, quite determined to get to the top of his profession.

1920s

Cousin Henry was seriously affected by the financial crises of the era.

1925

Thumbs up for the big race! Freddie poses in the family's racing colours.

1930s

Flossie liked to model the latest in hats, but otherwise cared little for fashion.

1940s

Charlie was a favourite among the ladies, and still has a merry twinkle in his eye!

1940s

Doris was a noted beauty of her time, with her lovely blonde colouring and large dark eyes.

1940s

A wicked grin characterizes her brother Bertie, something of a practical joker.

1950s

Alexandra, a lady of impeccable manners, was the family's first debutante.

1980s

Colour co-ordination was Coras strong point. Here she teams warm brown fur with a primrose cardigan.

1980

Her brother Nicholas thought such preoccupations rather beneath him!

1992

Oliver is a precocious infant for whom the family has great hopes.

1992

His cousin Thomas is proud to count such distinguished members among his famiily.

· Bear Tales ·

V.I.B s (Very Important Bears)

They Bear A Proud Name

Today, our cub reporter Junior has the privilege of interviewing some celebrity bears, though he's taking Uncle Barnaby with him for moral support. "Here they come now," he cries. "I'm so excited!" "Calm down, youngster," Barnaby reassures him. "Remember, they are just bears like you or me. Some were born great, like Alfonzo, some achieved greatness, like Red Bear and the Professor, and others had greatness thrust upon them, like Humphrey. But we were all born under the constellation of the Great Bear, so we meet as members of the same proud clan."

LEFT: Back in 1983, Humphrey, the bear of the then Prime Minister Margaret Thatcher, chats to a friendly bobby outside No. 10 Downing Street. It's not that he can't bear all that political talk indoors, but he's waiting for friends Annabel Bear and Fred the Ted before setting off on an outing, first to Mrs Thatcher's birthplace at Grantham, then on to a teddy bears' picnic at Belvoir Castle.

· The Professor ·

Back in 1972 a rather old and worn bear was offered for sale at a Michigan antique doll fair. There was little interest in bears at the time, so when Terry and Doris Michaud fell for his charm he became theirs for a mere fifteen dollars. Little did they guess what they had started! Once the Professor had trained them to appreciate the joy of bears, they became dedicated collectors – and the Professor is now known to bear lovers worldwide as the founder member of the famous Carrousel Museum collection of antique bears in Michigan.

V.I.Bs (Very Important Bears)

• Red Bear •

Neglected by his young English owners, Red Bear (below) was adopted by the Swiss nanny employed to teach the children French. *Le petit ours rouge* (the little red bear) now delights in reading story books in two languages with his friends the children.

• Alfonzo •

An aristocratic Russian Alfonzo (above) has blood as blue as his fur is red! Made by Steiff in 1908 for the Grand Duke of Russia's four-year-old daughter Princess Xenia Georgievna, he became her dearest friend – and a memento of her beloved father after the Duke's assassination in 1919. After her death in 1965, the imperial bear fetched a record price of £12,100 ($19,580) – and Steiff honoured him with a limited edition replica. Here he wears the Cossack tunic and trousers made for him by the princess's nanny.

LEFT: *Ready to climb every mountain, the glacier-grey Mount Everest Bear is a Merrythought special edition made for the fortieth anniversary of Sir Edmund Hillary's ascent of Mount Everest. He's not the only bear mountaineer. In 1965 Zissi the Bear accompanied Alpine climber Walter Bonatti up the North Face of the Matterhorn.*

· *Bear Tales* ·

MASCOT BEARS

Good Luck Bears

"Now I am going to tell you about the Great Bear Spirit," said Barnaby. "But I am afraid of ghosts!" trembled Junior. "No need to be afraid of this one," smiled Barnaby. "Ancient priests used to call for his aid before any noble undertaking. Since bears reminded people of this, they regarded teddy bears as mascots in all walks of life. The tradition of animal mascots escorting regiments into battle for luck is older than teddy bears themselves. But once teddies had arrived on the scene, they proved a lot more reliable than live animals, and were adopted far and wide as popular mascots both in the armed services and in civilian life."

ABOVE: Naturally, a Sandhurst bear does not buy his uniform off the peg. As befits his position, Edward's uniform was specially made for him by the Gentleman's Outfitters, Moss Bros in London. His parachute was also custom-made, in this case by the Royal Air Force Parachute School.

• *Senior Under Officer Edward Bear* •

In 1990 Edward retired from his post as mascot of the Parachuting Club of the Royal Military Academy, Sandhurst in Britain. In forty years of service he made more than 400 parachute jumps, accompanying most of the NATO armies at one time or another, and emerged with credit from kidnapping attempts by students. He went out in great style, ending his career with a sponsored jump for charity off the Hilton Hotel in London, before welcoming a younger bear as his successor.

MASCOT BEARS

• Rugby Mascot Bear •

Play ball with me and I'll play ball with you, says this tough-looking bruin (below). An early Steiff (c. 1904-1909), he was the prized mascot of the Gainsborough Rugby Team and attended all their matches. He claims they gave him the position of prop-forward, because he can bear down heavily in the scrum, though his smart rugby boots do not look as if they have seen all that much wear! Like many mascots, he wears his team's colours and boasts a full, miniature rugby kit. He does, however, have to play with a full-sized ball.

• Fire Guard Bear •

Stop the Home Fires burning! Mascot to the London Fire Brigade during the Blitz in World War II, this rare 1906 centre-seam Steiff (above) survived scores of firefighting missions almost unscathed. Note his Fire Brigade armband, marked 'bomb reconnaissance'.

LEFT: These endearing little fellows are Steiff miniatures, who served as pocket-sized mascots for pilots on flying missions during World War I. Their round glass eyes are positioned high on their heads to enable them to peep cheekily out of a breastpocket without running the risk of tumbling out!

INTERNATIONAL TEDDY BEARS

Bears Born Around The World

"Naturally," Barnaby continued, "once teddy bears had become established, other countries wanted to manufacture their own." "So they copied the American, German and British bears, I suppose," said Junior. "Not really," replied Barnaby. "These new manufacturers, in countries like Poland and, from World War II onwards, the Far East, recognized that the original bears were marvels of craftsmanship so they did not try to imitate them. They aimed at the other end of the market and made cheap mass-produced ranges, which they could then export to the Big Three bear producers." "So the better bear-breeders bought bears from the bad bear-breeder," joked Junior.

Barnaby frowned. "Certainly bears made outside the Big Three were inferior. Cheap cotton plush replaced mohair, jointing was cruder and some bears were even dangerous, as proved the case with some 1950s bears from Poland whose stuffing was made of noxious material. But these regrettably underbred bears became established as an economical alternative to home manufacture, and between the 1950s and 1970s actually put many established British, German and American firms out of business. Most popular were swarms of little yellow Polish bears, unjointed and made from cotton plush stuffed with hard straw with wire supports. Further upmarket were small, jointed, mohair 'Mutzi' bears from Switzerland, the rather fine plush Berg Brothers bears from Austria, and traditional British-style plush bears made by several firms in Australia. More recently, the introduction of safety standards has seen an improvement in mass-produced bears, and today they may fairly be said to complement, rather than undercut, the traditional and artist bears still produced by the Big Three."

FAR LEFT: This Dutch bear from the 1950s-1960s has a comical broad face, stumpy limbs and large, painted metal eyes. He is made of cheap cotton plush, with contrasting pads.

LEFT: The teddy craze gave rise to many postcards, now highly collectable.

RIGHT: Mass-produced imports can be hard to identify since many carry no maker's tag. This Austrian bear resembles the Zotty bears introduced by Steiff in 1951. His right ear sports the label of the Fechter Company.

INTERNATIONAL TEDDY BEARS

FAR LEFT: As teddies continued to dance across the world, the 1950s saw yet more countries entering the mass-produced bear market.

LEFT: For all her fine feathers, this little lady is no aristocrat but one of many mass-produced bears made for export in Israel in the 1950s.

ABOVE: This Swedish family, made by Anne-Marie Westberg in the 1980s, can boast blue blood of a kind. Their fabric may be unusual for teddy bears, but it is traditional in Sweden – for mattress covers!

BELOW: "I love these two Chinese bears in their felt jackets and trousers and stout plastic boots," said Junior. "China began producing this type of bear in the late 1940s" said Barnaby. "They have round faces, square noses, big round ears and big, three-clawed paws."

French Teddy Bears

They Dance In France

In 1903, France already had a long-established tradition of mechanical toy animals, including bears. To begin with, teddies were imported from Germany, but when World War I prevented trade across the border..." "They started making their own!" interrupted Junior. Barnaby continued, "French teddies generally fell short of the high standards set by the Germans and Americans, with inferior quality mohair or rayon plush (often brightly coloured), crude external jointing and insecurely attached eyes. Features include a narrow body with minimal hump, straight limbs and large, high-set ears. The best craftsmanship was reserved for mechanical bears that danced, played instruments or performed circus tricks."

ABOVE AND TOP RIGHT: France is justly famous for its mechanical bears. This polar bear made by the great Roullet & de Camp firm in c.1930 pours and 'drinks' a glass of wine. The dancing bear was made by Fernand Martin in c.1897.

CENTRE: Three typical French 1930s teddies with short mohair, narrow bodies and very basic joints.

RIGHT: A rare bear with the bat-shaped nose and metal button (inset) of FADAP, or Fabrique Artistique d'Animaux en Peluche ('Artistically Made Plush Animals'), in existence from 1920 until the 1970s.

BELOW: A bear made by the Jan Jac company of Paris (left) and a very early French bear, dated c. 1919 (centre).

Russian Teddy Bears

From Russia With Love

The Russian Bear may glower in political cartoons, but here we see a softer aspect. Teddies have never been a major industry in Russia, but it has produced both automated bears and soft toys since World War II, perhaps inspired by the popular folklore figure of Mishka the Bear.

ABOVE: Three rather wistful Russian bears made in the 1950s. They are fashioned of cotton plush and have round heads with big, low-set ears, a broad face gusset, horizontally stitched noses and traditional inverted V mouths. The arms are short and blunt, with teardrop-shaped pads. The legs are medium length, only one bear having well defined feet. All paws have simple embroidered claws.

Clockwork bears remained popular. The examples here fall midway between realistic and soft toy design, the bodies retaining a stylized naturalism but the heads being more teddy-like.

RIGHT: A merry balalaika player of c. 1955.

TOP RIGHT: 1977 produced a less frivolous character set to help in the kitchen pounding his pestle and mortar. These bears have a metal frame covered with cotton plush.

Japanese Teddy Bears

From The Land Of The Rising Sun

"Post-war Japan rarely neglected any manufacturing opportunity, and the teddy bear market was no exception," said Barnaby. "Cheap Japanese imported bears first hit the world market in the 1920s and proved popular. Quality was not a prime concern: cheap materials are characteristic, as are manufacturing shortcuts including inferior wire jointing and 'sliced-in ears' inserted in holes cut in the head and glued in place. Straight, narrow bodies and limbs and small, round feet recall the cheaper American and European ranges. From the 1950s, Japan became the world's leader in the automated tin toy industry and turned this ingenuity to clockwork or battery-operated bears. Twenty years later, Japanese manufacturers successfully invaded the lower end of the cuddly toy market with machine-made, unjointed bears in synthetic fabrics. Later, increasing westernization produced the first Japanese Teddy Bear Fair in 1985." "So will they ever make artist bears?" asked Junior. "Who knows," said Barnaby. "If there is enough interest in American artist bears, perhaps they will."

LEFT: Two mechanical bears from the 1950s have cloth and nylon plush bodies over a tin frame.

BELOW: A 1940s bear made of wool plush has unusual embroidered black eyes.

ABOVE : A Japanese bear from the 1940s shows the enormous 'sliced-in' ears (with interior wire supports!) and rather nice airbrushed claws characteristic of Japanese bears of this period.

LEFT: An early Japanese bear, attributed to the 1920s, is made of synthetic plush with velveteen paws and tiny felt ears. The vertically stitched nose and long inverted V mouth are typically Japanese.

Australian Teddy Bears

Bears From Down Under

"Imported teddy bears were marketed in Australia from 1908," said Barnaby, "but homebred bears had to wait until 1920 when the Joy Toy Company of Melbourne added teddies to their range. Other firms followed suit, including Emil Toys (1933-1980s), Verna Toys (1941-1980s), and the Berlex Company (1950s-1970s). Early Aussies were fully jointed, in quality mohair with glass eyes. Shortage of materials during World War II saw the arrival of sheepskin bears, and produced a distinctively Australian type: a bear who saved on card and metal by doing without a neck joint." "I bet he had a stiff neck," joked Junior. "Cheap Asian imports drove many firms out of the market in the 1970s. Other companies kept going with Australian-designed bears assembled in Asia, and recently several small firms have successfully produced collectors' bears."

TOP, ABOVE AND LEFT: Four 1930s bears made by Joy Toys. The teddy in the hat (top) gives us a good view of the nose favoured by several Australian firms, including Joy Toys and Emil: broad and vertically stitched with the outer stitches extended upwards. Joy Toys was sold to British owners in 1966, to become one of the firms driven out of business by Asian imports; perhaps it is in sympathy with their manufacturers that the two bears above have taken to their bed. Our last example (left) looks as if he has a better claim to the bed, but through thick and thin he has preserved the embroidered Joy Toys label on his right foot.

COLLECTABLE BEARS TODAY

The New Wave Bears

"When collectors increase and the number of antique bears does not, what do bear-makers do?" "asked Barnaby. "Grin and bear it?" suggested Junior. "Obviously, they need to produce new ranges of collectables, and from the late 1970s that's just what they did. The New Wave Bears, made in limited editions to ensure they do not become too common, come in four classes. There are the Old Guard, lovingly made replicas of golden oldies which several long-established firms have been able to recreate from their archives. They are made from the same materials as the originals and, where appropriate, with the same techniques such as hand-embroidered noses. There are Artists' Bears, designed and hand-made by teddy bear artists in every style from traditional to wild and whacky. There are Anniversary Bears, made (often as Artists' Bears) to honour the 'birthdays' of old (and sometimes much younger) firms. And finally there are Character Bears, complete with personality and background." "Like the Wareham Bears and Vanderbears," said Junior. "And my favourites Humphrey Beargart and Amelia Bearhart!"

ABOVE LEFT: Teddy Blue was Steiff's first replica made for members of the Steiff Club, in 1992. He is a copy of their Teddy Baby series, which was popular from 1930 to the 1950s, though his predecessors came in a wider range of colours, including white, beige and pinky brown.

ABOVE RIGHT: His companion is Hermann's 75th Anniversary Bear. Specially commissioned in 1990, he is made of traditional materials (mohair, with felt pads and wood wool stuffing) to appeal to collectors.

BELOW: The little patriots in red, white and blue were produced in limited edition by Merrythought in 1992 to celebrate the 40th anniversary of Queen Elizabeth II's coronation. They are replicas of Merrythought's original Coronation Bear of 1953.

ABOVE: The North American Bear Company's 'Vanderbear' family are stars in the Character Bear world. Little Muffy Vanderbear has a star-sized wardrobe. Here she models a mere three of her fifty outfits – Wild West, Dutch and ballet costumes.

BLE BEARS TODAY

LEFT: Pamela Ann Howells designed bears for the Chiltern label from 1958 to 1968, but is today known in her own right as one of Britain's leading modern bear artists. Benjie is one of her creations. Made in 1992, he blends a modern image with respect for traditional techniques and materials.

BELOW: Dressed up in her Sunday best, but for all her old-fashioned charm, Jennifer is a 1992 creation by American bear artist Sandy Fleming. Her lace-edged frock and frilly bonnet reflect the growing market for elaborately costumed bears.

LEFT: American bear artist Sue Lain takes pains to ensure that each of her bears has an individual and appealing expression. The freshness and charm of her creations appears in Abbey, with her delightful straw bonnet, and dungaree-clad Albert, on his way home from picking blueberries. Abbey is supplied with a dress made from vintage material.

BEAR CARE

Save Our Bears

"You will note," said Barnaby sternly, "the need for people to take care of their bears. Whether expensive antiques or artist bears, or childhood friends, teddies deserve responsible treatment." Junior agreed, and offered a poetic guide to bear care. "Wear and tear is tough on a bear. He needs tender care – or else beware: you'll have to repair!"

PROTECTING Remember to pick up your bear by the body, not by an arm or an ear. Mishandling will break up the stuffing, leaving a saggy arm or loose ear. Try to keep your bear in an even temperature, and avoid strong sunlight, which fades the fur. Dressed bears in particular end up two-tone! An expensive antique is best housed in a glass-fronted cabinet, or at least dressed to protect the mohair – also good protection for much-loved and worn bears.

ABOVE: A common complaint in the well-loved bear is the saggy arm, caused by a loving owner always holding the teddy by the same arm till the stuffing gives way!

REPAIRING Major repairs require professional surgery, but minor ones can be done at home. The most common areas of wear on a teddy bear are the pads and paws. It is a good idea to cover worn pads with a piece of felt, slightly larger than the original, stitched securely round the outer edge. This will prevent any further loss of stuffing. It will also preserve the original pad until it can be replaced or repaired professionally. For another stopgap measure, remember that it pays to check all the bear's seams from time to time. You can easily insert a few small stitches where needed: as the saying goes, a stitch in time saves nine!

LEFT AND RIGHT: Dressing up helps protect the bear's mohair against light and dust. You may choose to use antique doll's clothing, small children's clothes, or make your own costumes.

BEAR CARE

REPAIRING Facial repairs are often easier than they sound. Replacement eyes (shoebutton or glass) can be bought and stitched on from the outside. Safety eyes are also available, but fitting is more complicated and requires the removal of the bear's head. For a child's bear, a simple substitute for safety eyes is an old trouser button with four holes, sewn on extra securely. Noses, mouths and claws can be re-stitched in twisted thick embroidery silk or wool, if possible marking out the original outline in tailor's chalk before removing the old thread.

LEFT: The most battered of bears can still be saved by the expert bear restorer, who may not be able to make him look brand new but can restore his dignity. And you may find yourself with a bear of such noble lineage as an early Steiff!

STORING If you need to store your bear, never put him in a polythene bag, which will draw moisture to him. A brown paper parcel is ideal, as this will let the bear 'breathe'. A sturdy cardboard box filled with tissue paper is also suitable. Never store an unprotected teddy in a loft or cupboard: it is an open invitation to moths and other insects to burrow their way into his fabric and lay their eggs there, causing great damage. And damp sheds or garages are certainly to be avoided. The moisture will make a bear's stuffing coagulate into lumps and rust the metal pins in his joints so they no longer move.

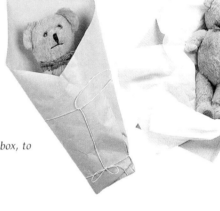

RIGHT: Wrap your bear up securely in a brown paper parcel, or store him in a cardboard box, to protect him from the ravages of moths and other insects.

CLEANING A new bear only needs occasional brushing with a soft brush. But if your bear needs cleaning, you can do this yourself. You need two bowls of warm water and two additional soft brushes. To one bowl add a capful of a washing liquid for soft fabrics or wool, and whisk it into foam. After gently brushing your bear with his normal brush to remove any dust, take one of the other brushes and apply a little of the foam– not the water – to his surface, using circular movements. When all the bear has been treated, rinse him off with the final brush, dipped into the bowl of clear water. Shake off any excess water and gently work over the bear, in circles, until the foam has gone. If you get his surface at all wet, dab it off immediately with a soft towel. Leave the bear to dry in a natural surrounding, never in an airing cupboard or anywhere too warm.

ABOVE LEFT: Brush the bear gently with a baby brush to remove any dust in the pile.

ABOVE RIGHT: Use only foam to clean the bear, brushing with gentle, circular movements.

MAKING AN HEIRLOOM BEAR

♥

Make your own jointed teddy bear

The choice of fabric is very important in determining the final look of your bear. These bears are all made from the same basic pattern but the different fabrics and lengths of pile affect the appearance of each bear.

Making your own bear will give you enormous pleasure and satisfaction. A hand-made bear becomes a very special heirloom if given as a gift or, if you collect bears, the bear created by you will take pride of place in your hug.

When making your first bear it helps to have some degree of dressmaking skill but it is not absolutely necessary. If you do not have dressmaking experience, have a go using a woven-backed synthetic fur with a pile between 5–10 mm (³⁄₈–¹⁄₂"). This will be easier to handle and not nearly as costly as using mohair.

Teddy bears made for children should conform to local safety standards. Buy your materials and filling from a supplier selling components conforming to the required standard and use plastic safety eyes which are properly fixed with a safety washer (when the bear is finished you should not be able to get your nails under the eyes). The pattern has been simplified as much as possible. Before buying materials, however, read the instructions carefully several times over.

Materials

30 cm (12 in) Teddy Bear

25 cm (10 in) of woven fabric 140 cm (54") wide

3 x 36 mm (1^1/$_2$") disc/cotter pin joint assembly sets

2 x 25 mm (1") disc/cotter pin joint assembly sets

1 pair 10–12 mm safety eyes

35 cm (14 in) Teddy Bear

30 cm (12") of woven fabric 140 cm (54") wide

5 x 36 mm (1^1/$_2$") disc/cotter pin joint assembly sets

1 pair 12–13.5 mm safety eyes

43 cm (17 in) Teddy Bear

40 cm (16") of woven fabric 140 cm (54") wide

2 x 36 mm (1^1/$_2$") disc/cotter pin joint assembly sets

3 x 50 mm (2") disc/cotter pin joint assembly sets

1 pair 14–15.5 mm safety eyes

All Bears

1 reel extra-strong matching button thread

1 reel of matching heavy-weight machine-sewing thread

1 heavy-duty sewing-machine needle

1 long darning needle

1 pair long-nosed pliers with a fine point

1 pair sharp thin-bladed scissors approx. 16 cm (6") long

1 knitting needle or skewer

Dark-brown or black embroidery thread

15 x 20.5 cm (6 x 8") square of soft suede, leather, heavy-weight wool felt, velvet or upholstery fabric

225 g (^{1}/$_2$ lb) high-quality polyester filling

Wooden spoon handle or piece of dowelling for stuffing

1 black permanent ink pen

1 sheet thin card 70 x 50 cm (27 x 20") or several cereal boxes

1 glue stick

glass headed pins

Templates for the bear pattern are found on pages 148–151. For the 35 cm (14 in) bear, either photocopy each template twice, or make two tracings of each template, discarding one centre head panel in each case. Cut out each template and stick onto thin card, leaving at least 5 cm (^{1}/$_2$") between the pattern pieces. Draw a 6 mm (^{1}/$_4$") seam allowance round each template. Make a hole at the fixing points marked on the head, leg and arm templates. Mark the positions of the darts. Do not cut into the darts. Mark the direction of the arrows on the underside of one pattern piece in each pair.

MAKING AN HEIRLOOM BEAR

To make the 30 cm (12") bear you will need to reduce the templates to 85% on a photocopier.

To make the 43 cm (17") bear you will need to enlarge the templates to 115% on a photocopier.

Important: Remember to add a 6 mm (¼") seam allowance around each template.

You should now have nineteen pattern pieces with one centre head panel and nine pairs of limb, head and body pattern pieces.

1 Determine the direction of the pile of the fabric by stroking it to find which direction smoothes it down.

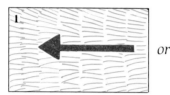 *or*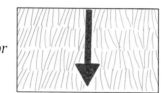

Mark the fabric on the wrong side with an arrow showing the direction in which you stroked. Refer tot he layouts on pp. 150–151 to lay down the pattern pieces, making sure that the arrows on both fabric and pattern run in the same direction. One piece in each pair of patterns should be reversed to form a mirror image of its fellow.

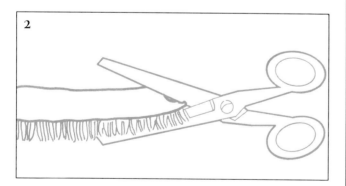

2 Draw round each pattern piece, holding the card firmly in place. Cut out each piece. When cutting fur fabric, cut only the backing, avoiding cutting the pile by sliding the bottom blade of the scissors forward between the fibres and keeping the blade in contact with the backing all the time. Do not cut into the darts.

The pattern pieces for the paw and foot pads should be laid down on the chosen fabric in a similar way.

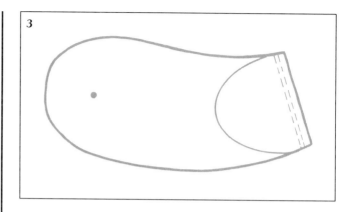

3 With right sides together, pin, tack and double stitch each paw to the matching inner side arms, taking care to match D to D and E to E.

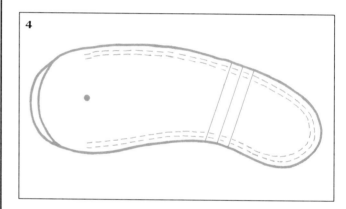

4 With right sides together, pin the inner and outer arms together and tack. Leaving a gap between the two points X at the top of the arm, double stitch along the seam lines.

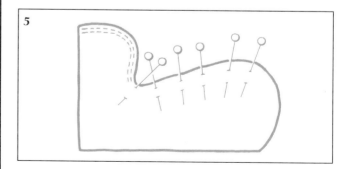

MAKING AN HEIRLOOM BEAR

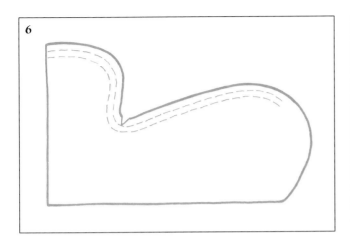

6 Snip halfway through the seam allowance at the angle of foot and leg.

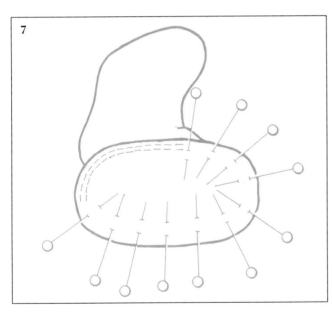

7 Fit the foot pads to the legs, matching F to F and G to G. Pin, tack and stitch the pad in place. Turn the leg right side out

8 Take the two body side pieces and, with right sides together, match up the head positions at point H. Smooth the two pieces together until you have a perfect fit. Pin, tack and double stitch, leaving an opening between the points marked X. This opening will be used to fix the head and limbs to the body and to stuff the body cavity. Turn the body right side out.

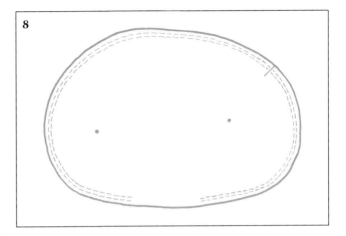

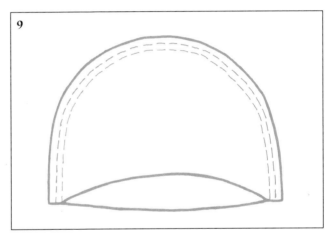

9 With right sides together, pin the ear pieces together in pairs, leaving the bottom open. Tack and double stitch all round the curve. Turn right side out.

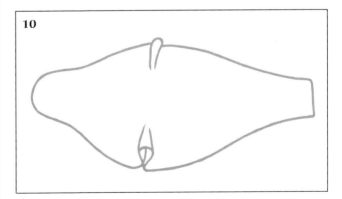

10 Pin, tack and double stitch each dart on the centre head panel with right sides together.

MAKING AN HEIRLOOM BEAR

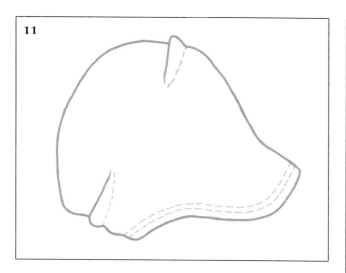

11 On each of the two head side panels, double stitch the darts at the crown and at the neck of the head. Pin together the two head side panels matching A to A and C to C. Tack and stitch from A to C.

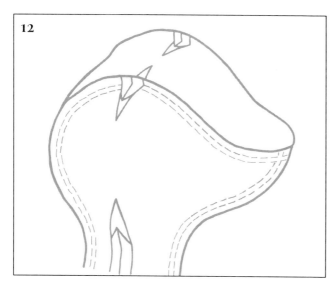

12 Open out the head side panels. Take the centre head panel and pin the point A to the point A where the head side panels join. All right sides should be facing inwards. Match the darts in the centre head panel with those at the crown of the head side panels and pin. Ease the panels to fit, matching B to B at the back neck edge. Tack and double stitch the three head panels together, leaving free the neck opening from C to B. You may find it easier to hand sew the nose area using a small back stitch. Turn right side out.

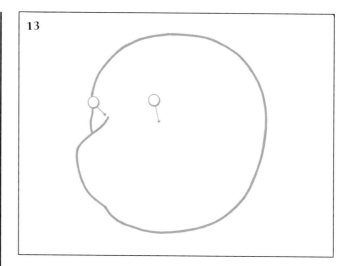

13 Lightly fill the head with stuffing so that the shape is visible. Try out suitable positions for the eyes by inserting two glass-headed pins. Mark the chosen positions with permanent ink pen and remove the temporary filling.

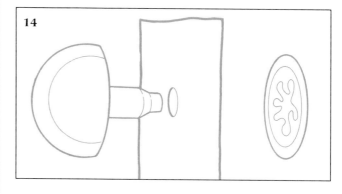

14 Make a hole at each eye position with a knitting needle. Push the stem of the eye through the hole. From the inside of the head, place the metal washer over the stem, with the teeth pointing away from the eye, and push it firmly towards the eye.

15 Begin stuffing the head at the nose. Push small pieces of filling into the nose, building up the shape slowly and evenly and firming it in with the handle of a wooden spoon or piece of dowelling. Continue with the rest of the head, starting at the crown. Check that all parts of the head are well and evenly stuffed, especially the nose area. In general, the more stuffing material used, the firmer the bear will be and the better it will keep its shape.

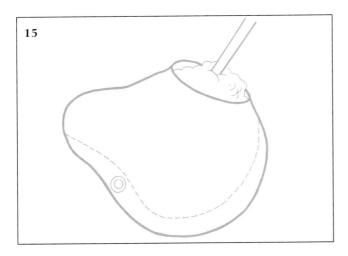

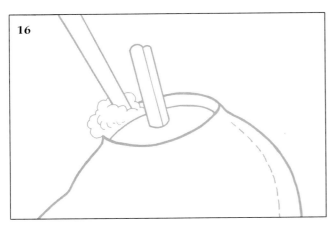

16 Take a cotter pin and place on it a washer followed by a disc (use the larger sized discs for the 30 cm (12") and 43 cm (17") bears). Turn the head upside down and lay the disc and cotter pin on top of the stuffing.

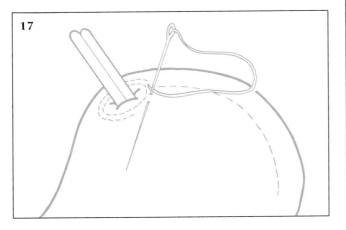

17 Sew a double button-thread running stitch around the neck and pull up tightly over the disc, leaving the cotter pin protruding. Sew back and forth across the gathered neck until all is firm. Fasten off securely.

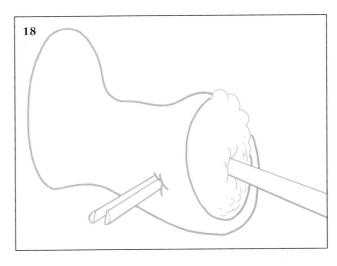

18 Stuff the arms and legs in the same way. Half fill each one, taking care to stuff the paws and feet firmly. Assemble a cotter pin, washer and disc as before, using the larger-sized discs for the legs. From the inside of the limb, make a hole where marked. Push the cotter pin through the hole from the inside.

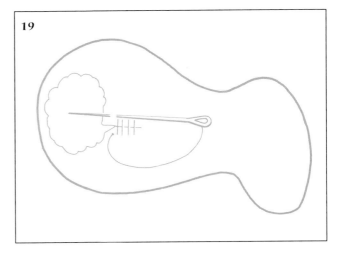

19 Finish stuffing the limb and close off the opening with ladder stitch, using double button thread and pulling the stitching tightly. Make sure the turnings are tucked into the seam.

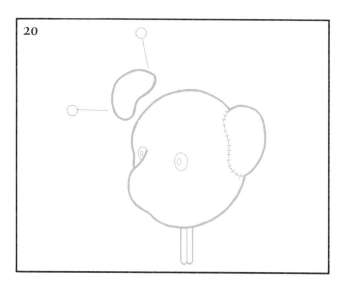

20 Turn in 6 mm (¼") around the raw edges of the ears and tack together. Place the ears on the head in a position you are happy with and pin to the head. Ladder stitch around the ears, using button thread.

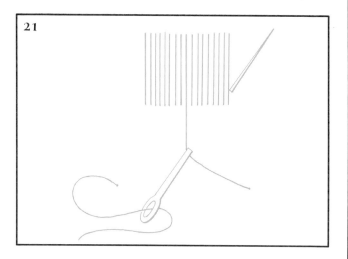

21 Using black or dark brown embroidery thread, sew four claws onto the feet and paws. Use matching thread to embroider the nose with horizontal or vertical satin stitches. For the mouth, do not finish off the stitching at the nose but, with plenty of thread on the needle, insert the needle at one end of the mouth and bring it out at the other, leaving the thread in a loop on the first side. Insert the needle again inside the loop at the centre point of the mouth. Bring the needle out at the side of the nose, draw up the thread and finish off the nose neatly.

22 Push a knitting needle through the seam of the body at the point H, making sure that it goes through the centre of the seam. Take the head and push its cotter pin down through this hole in the body. Place a disc and then a washer onto the pin on the inside of the body. Push the halves of the pin apart. Grip one side of the pin with long-nosed pliers and bend it into a spiral. Do the same with the other side, making sure that both spirals are pressing down hard on the washer. Check the joint for tightness and adjust if necessary. Attach the limbs to the body in a similar way, using the positions marked on the templates to position the joints correctly.

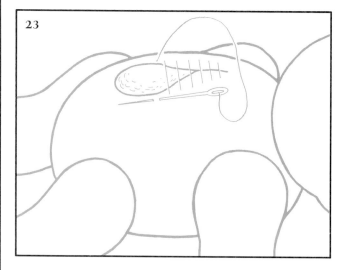

23 Firmly stuff all areas of the body, attending especially to the neck, shoulders, groin and undercarriage. Close the back with ladder stitching and comb out all the seams.

Dressing the Bears

Scarf (30 cm (12") bear)

Materials
9 x 38 cm (3¹/₂ x 15") strip of fine cotton
    stockinet
1 skein matching no. 5 pearl cotton

Fold the fabric in half with right sides together. Stitch around the edges, leaving a gap in the middle of one edge. Turn and slip stitch closed. Cut the pearl cotton into 8 cm (3") lengths and, at the ends of the scarf, hook through three or four strands at a time, using a fine crochet hook. Knot each set and cut the fringe level.

Dress (35 cm (14") bear)

Materials
50 cm (¹/₂ yd) dress fabric
Bias binding
Matching machine thread
1 small button
Lace or ric rac braid (optional)

Use the templates on p. 153 to cut out the pattern pieces, placing the dress front to the fold of the fabric. With right sides together, sew the centre back seams together up to the dot. Make a placket at the back opening. With right sides together, pin, tack and sew the front and back side seams and the sleeve seams. Matching notches at the armholes, sew the sleeves and dress together at the armholes. Sew two rows of running stitches around the neck edge of the dress and sleeves and gather. Bind the neck with bias binding. Gather and bind the lower edge of the sleeve to fit the bear's arm. Sew on a closing button to the back of the dress. Sew a loop to the matching edge.

Waistcoat (43 cm (17") bear)

Materials
31 x 31 cm (12 x 12") square of good quality
    felt, fine leather or ultra-sued
3 small buttons

Use the templates on p. 152 to cut out the pattern pieces. Taking a 6 mm (¹/₄") seam allowance and with right sides together, join the shoulder and side seams. Press open by hand. Turn in a 3 mm (¹/₈") hem to the wrong side on the remaining raw edges of the waistcoat. Edge stitch by machine. Mark and cut three evenly-spaced holes on the left front of the waistcoat. Sew on the buttons.

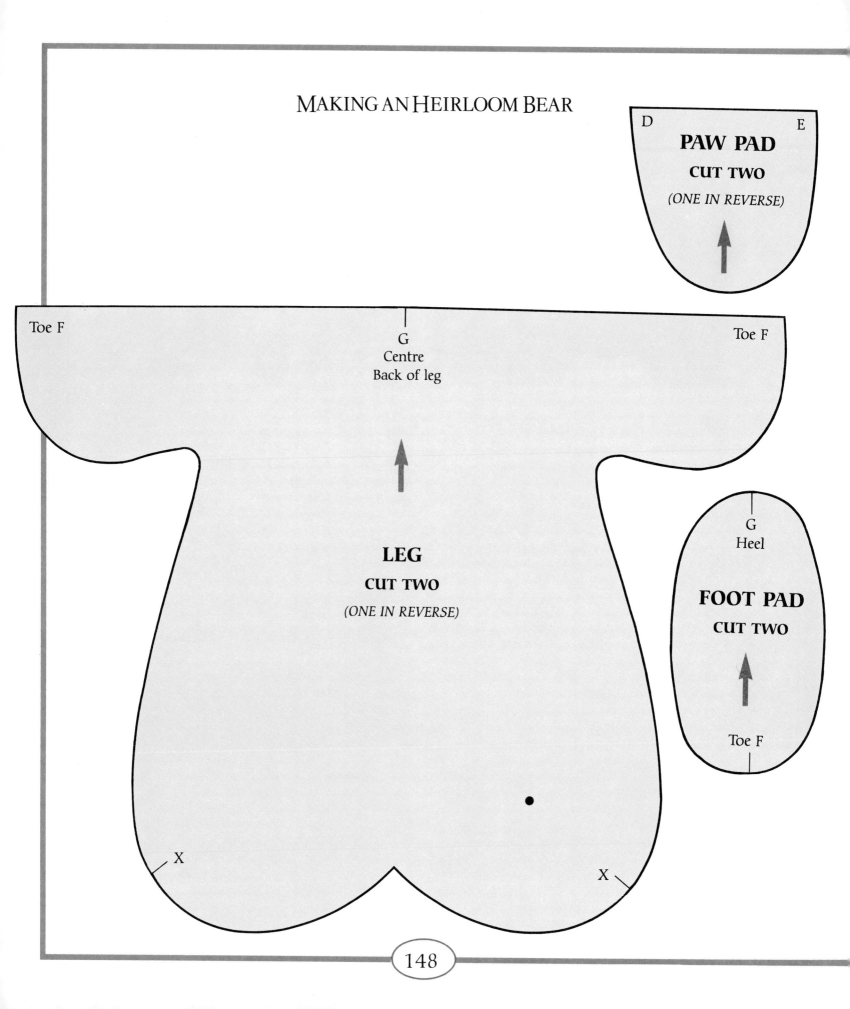

PAW PAD

CUT TWO

(ONE IN REVERSE)

D

E

Toe F

G
Centre
Back of leg

Toe F

LEG

CUT TWO

(ONE IN REVERSE)

X

X

G
Heel

FOOT PAD

CUT TWO

Toe F

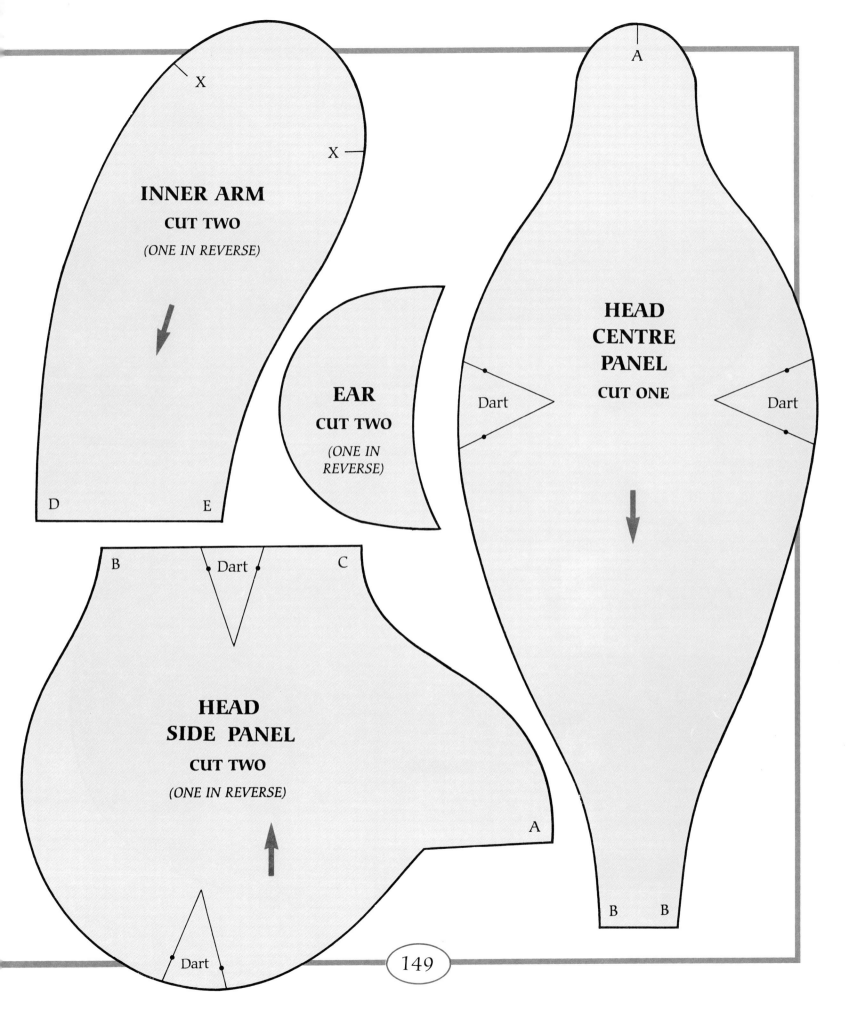

INNER ARM
CUT TWO
(ONE IN REVERSE)

X
X
D
E

EAR
CUT TWO
*(ONE IN
REVERSE)*

A

**HEAD
CENTRE
PANEL**
CUT ONE

Dart
Dart

B   B

B   C
Dart

**HEAD
SIDE PANEL**
CUT TWO
(ONE IN REVERSE)

A

Dart

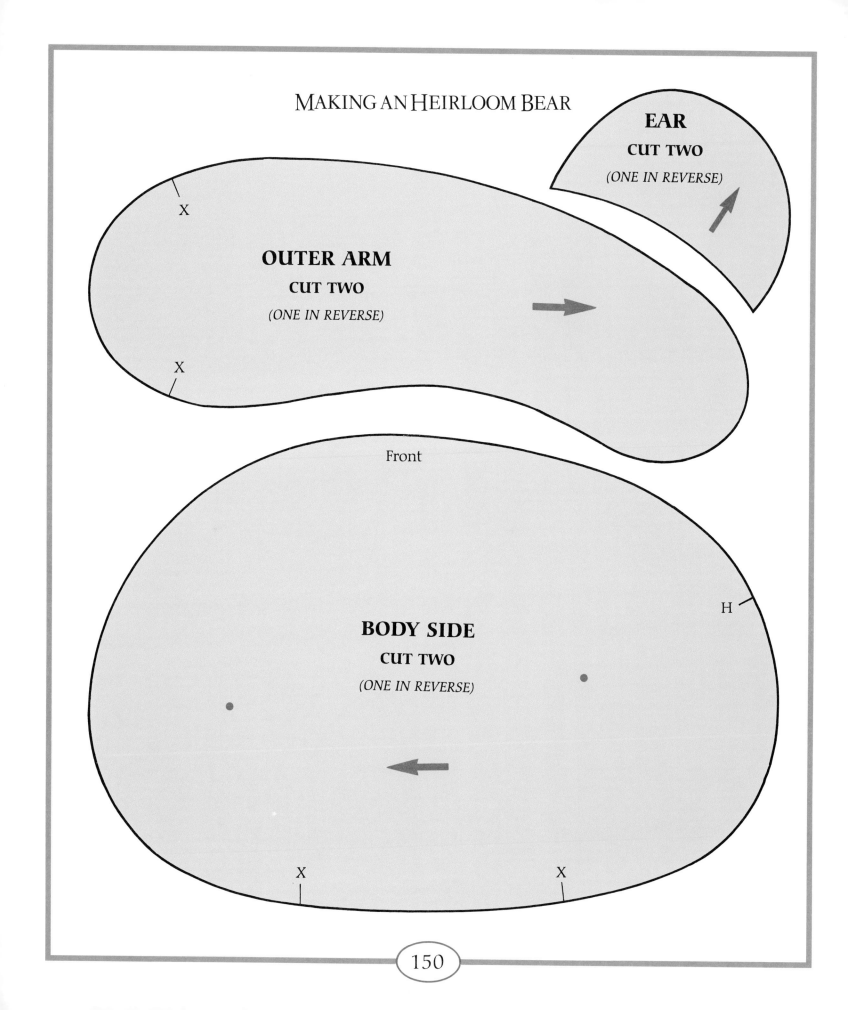

EAR

CUT TWO

(ONE IN REVERSE)

OUTER ARM

CUT TWO

(ONE IN REVERSE)

X

X

Front

H

BODY SIDE

CUT TWO

(ONE IN REVERSE)

X

X

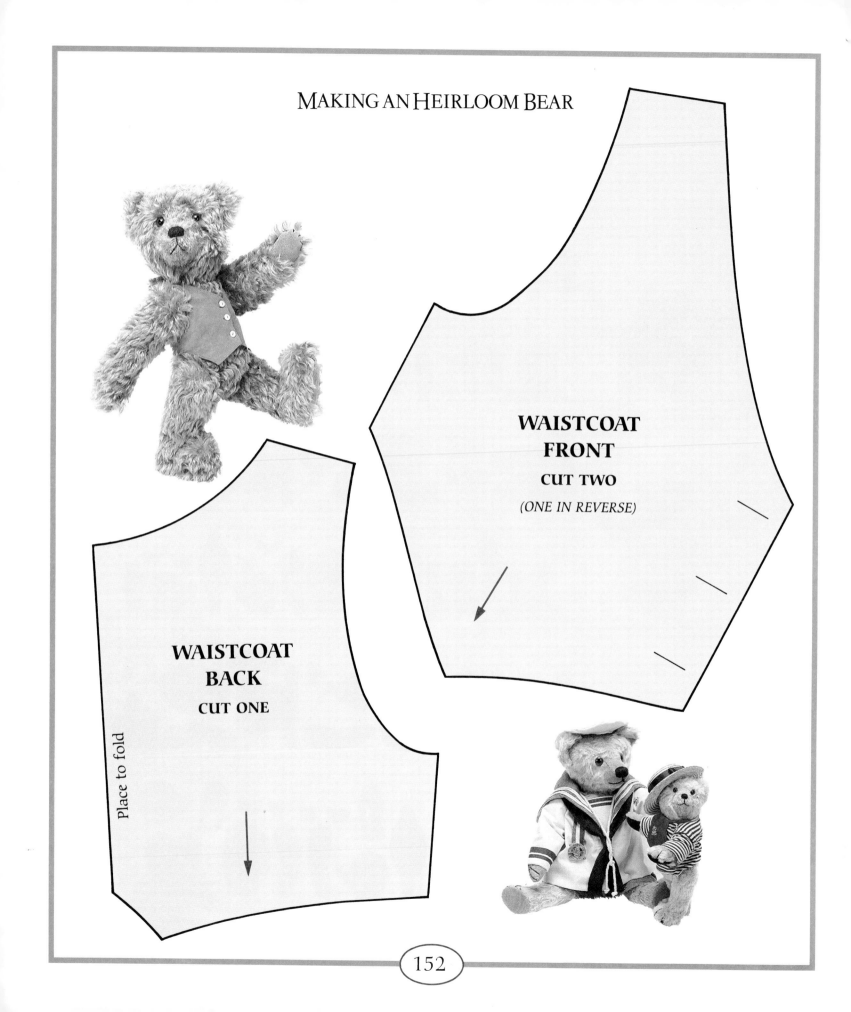

**WAISTCOAT
FRONT**

CUT TWO

(ONE IN REVERSE)

**WAISTCOAT
BACK**

CUT ONE

Place to fold

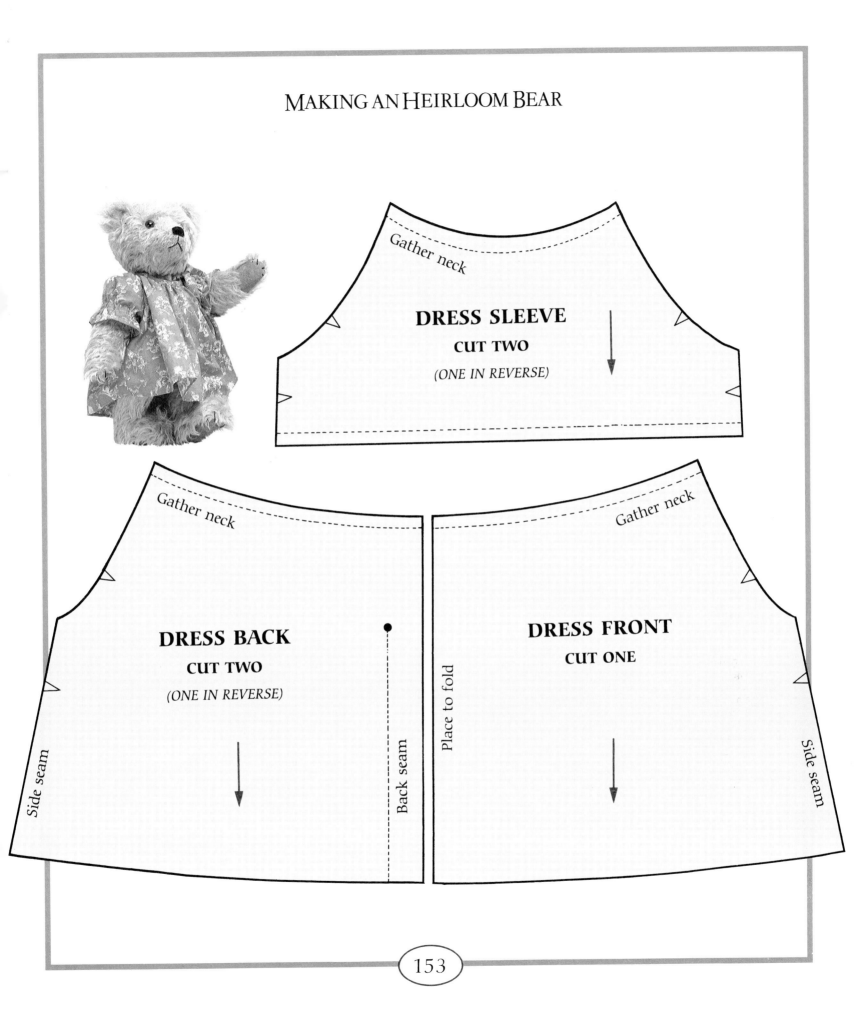

DRESS SLEEVE

CUT TWO

(ONE IN REVERSE)

Gather neck

DRESS BACK

CUT TWO

(ONE IN REVERSE)

Gather neck

Side seam

Back seam

Place to fold

DRESS FRONT

CUT ONE

Gather neck

Side seam

INDEX

INDEX

ACKNOWLEDGEMENTS

The authors and the publishers would like to thank the following for permitting their bears to be photographed and for their very generous assistance in the production of this book (teddy bear museums and shops are printed in bold):

Dottie Ayres 19, 24, 32, 35, 37, 39, 41, 42, 43, 44, 46, 47, 49, 62, 72, 74, 77, 85, 131; Brian Beacock 17, 18, 19, 73, 94, 99, 106, 107, 109, 110, 117, 121; 124, 125; **The Bear Garden, Guildford** 40, 122, 123, 136; **Michele Brandreth, The Teddy Bear Museum, 19 Greenhill Street, Stratford upon Avon** 22, 60, 66, 70, 86, 114, 132, 133, 134; Gina Campbell 82; Mrs S.J. Davies, Chatterbox, Midhurst, West Sussex 138; Peter and Frances Fagan, Colour Box Miniatures Ltd 48, 49, 50, 51, 83, 84, 85, 88, 114, 139; Francoise Flint 10, 14, 17, 19, 20, 27, 28, 30, 38, 42, 45, 46, 47, 54, 57, 60, 61, 64, 73, 80, 81, 94, 107, 124, 125, 132, 134, 138; Gerry Grey 17, 18, 19; **Paul Goble's Bears and Friends, 32 Meeting House Lane, Brighton** 29, 56, 62, 72, 110, 120, 138; Dee Hockenberry 46; Mary Holden, Only Natural, Tunbridge Wells, Kent 16, 17, 140–153; Oliver Holmes, Merrythought Ltd 92, 93, 95, 136; Wendy Lewis 26, 28, 30, 33, 49, 54, 56, 62, 63, 72, 74–75, 75, 79, 80, 81, 86, 88, 98, 99, 100, 101, 104, 105, 111, 118, 120, 124, 125, 127, 128, 131, 132, 134, 135, 138; **Terry and Doris Michaud, Carrousel, Chesaning, Michigan** 14, 19, 20, 21, 22, 23, 38, 29, 31, 32, 42, 44, 45, 46, 47, 52, 58, 62, 63, 73, 74, 75, 89, 96, 111, 119, 124, 125, 132, 136;

Sue Pearson 44, 65, 72, 78, 101; Roy Pilkington, Oakley Fabrics, 8 May Street, Luton, Bedfordshire 17, 18, 19; **Ian Pout, Teddy Bears of Witney, 99 High Street, Witney, Oxfordshire** 17, 22, 23, 25, 33, 38, 43, 54, 57, 58, 65, 68–69, 70, 100, 108, 111, 112, 115, 120, 133, 134, 135, 136, 137; **Judy Sparrow, The Bear Museum, 38 Dragon Street, Petersfield** 48, 52, 58–59, 64, 71, 73, 74, 75, 76, 80, 81, 86, 89, 92, 93, 96, 98, 99, 100, 101, 105, 106, 106, 108, 110, 112, 115, 116, 118, 124, 125, 131; **Maureen Stanford, Childhood Memories, Farnham Antique Centre, Farnham, Surrey** 17, 18, 19, 97, 113, 139; **David and Ankie Wild, Musuem of Childhood, Ribchester** 65, 69, 121, 131, 132, 133; Evelyn and Mort Wood 26, 28, 34, 45, 52, 53, 78, 79, 104, 112; Rosemary Volpp 10, 14, 24–25, 27, 32, 36, 38, 43, 45, 54, 61, 66, 73, 76.

Picture Credits: Bear Brand 14; Cobra and Bellamy, 149 Sloane St, London 14; The Dean's Company 112; Peter and Frances Fagan, Colour Box Miniatures Ltd, East End Lauder, Berwickshire 88; Gebrüder Hermann GmbH & Co. KG 16; Gerry Grey 15; Courtesy of the National Museum of the American Indian 10; The Royal Military Academy Sandhurst 126; Smithsonian Institute, New York 12; Topham Picture Source 82; Roosevelt Centre 10; Steiff; 13, 58; Rosemary Volpp 10, 76; Rose Wharnsby 11, 14, 52, 86, 130.